ELITE SERIES

EDITOR: MARTIN WINDROW

Israeli Elite Units since 1948

Text by SAMUEL M. KATZ

Colour plates by RON VOLSTAD

OSPREY PUBLISHING LONDON

Dedication
To the paratroop fallen in the Jordan Valley, and
their families—whose sacrifice allowed others to live
in peace.

Published in 1988 by
Osprey Publishing Ltd
Member company of the George Philip Group
12–14 Long Acre, London WC2E 9LP
© Copyright 1988 Osprey Publishing Ltd

British Library Cataloguing in Publication Data

Katz, Samuel
    Israeli elite units since 1948—(Elite
    series 18)
    1. Israel—Armed Forces—History
    I. Title   II. Series
    355.3′5′095694   UA 853.I8

    ISBN 085045 8374

Filmset in Great Britain
Printed through Bookbuilders Ltd, Hong Kong

Author's Note
The author wishes to thank the following for their
invaluable assistance during the preparation of this
book: Mr Joseph S. Bermudez Jr., Mr Lee E. Russel
Miki K., Bat-Sheva, Harry Sturmwind, the staff at
the IDF Archives, Maj. Dvora Takson of the IDF
Spokesmen, and very special thanks to Mr Andreas
Constantinou, for his always available technical
assistance. Last but not least to my wife Sigalit, who
love and extreme patience under the most nerve-
racking of conditions made this book possible.

Readers are referred to Elite 8, *Israeli Defence Forces
Since 1973*; Men-at-Arms 165, *Armies in Lebanon
1982–84*; and MAA 194, *Arab Armies of the Middle Eas
Wars (2)*, all of which contain material
complementary to this book.

Artist's Note
Readers may care to note that the original paintings
from which the colour plates in this book were
prepared are available for private sale. All
reproduction copyright whatsoever is retained by the
publisher. All enquiries should be addressed to:
    Ronald B. Volstad
    PO Box 1577
    Main Post Office
    Edmonton
    Alberta
    Canada T5J 2N9
The publishers regret that they can enter into no
correspondence upon this matter.

Editor's Note
Since written Hebrew script does not distinguish
between capitals and 'lower case' characters in the
European manner, direct transliterations of Hebrew
titles and terms are printed in SMALL CAPITALS
throughout the text. Since Anglicised Hebrew uses
mainly American, rather than British spellings, this
convention has been maintained here.

The First Military Elite

Ve are here to found a Jewish Army.'
Capt. Orde Wingate, 13 September 1938: SNS
Jewish Sergeants' Course, Kibbutz Ein Herod.

1929, and later in 1936, Palestinian Arabs
itiated violent riots against the Jews and British to
rther their own nationalistic aspirations. In 1929
e HAGANAH (Israel's 'pre-statehood' underground
my) found itself incapable of conducting military
perations beyond low-level defensive efforts. In
336, accepting that they did not possess the means
ccessfully to defend Jewish life and property, the
itish established a special Jewish Police Force or
TRIM ('Guards'), which consisted of 'Super-
imerary Police' and highly mobile 'Settlement
plice'. Virtually every NOTER was a member of the
GANAH, and a careful balance between divided
yalties ensued. The 'Settlement Police' were
anipulated by the HAGANAH into an élite force.
heir 'illegal' commander was Yitzhak Sadeh, a
ilitary visionary, who trained the NODEDOT—as
ey became known—in the art of unconventional
arfare. The NODEDOT specialised in mobility and
rprise attacks; the Arabs feared them greatly. The
TRIM provided the HAGANAH with its cadre of
mbat-experienced personnel, attracting the élite
Palestine's Jewish youth—men like Moshe
ayan and Yigal Allon, who began their military
reers as NOTRIM.
The riots of 1936 and the establishment of the
TRIM broadened the outlook of the HAGANAH;
d 1937 saw the establishment of the FO'SH
Iebrew abbreviation for PLUGOT SADEH or 'Field
ompanies'). The FO'SH was a mobilised élite strike
rce whose members were hand-picked by Yitzhak
deh for their intelligence, strength and ded-

A Special Night Squad led by a British NCO set out from Kibbutz Hanita to patrol along the Iraq Petroleum Pipeline, September 1938. Note variety of civilian and military dress worn, as well as assortment of SMLEs and shotguns carried. (HAGANAH Archives)

ication. Sadeh was the ideal commander for such a force; his eccentric but comforting uncon- ventionality earned the devotion of his men, and the affectionate nickname of 'HAZAKEN', the 'Old Man'.

The FO'SH became the commando arm of the HAGANAH; and an entity unto itself. Sadeh created FO'SH topographical and educational units, as well as a small but extremely effective Arabic-speaking intelligence service. By March 1938 the FO'SH boasted over 1,500 fully trained fighters divided into 13 regional groups. They carried stolen and semi-legal British SMLEs, grenades and rifles 'liberated' from Arab guerrillas, and some small arms produced in improvised HAGANAH armaments factories. The FO'SH openly confronted the Arabs in battle, attacking their villages in swift raids, taking full advantage of their mobility. The Arabs, used to

3

unco-ordinated mob attacks, could not defeat the FO'SH in battle.

Between 1936 and 1939, hundreds of Jewish 'stockade and tower' settlements were set up to populate areas throughout Palestine. One observer impressed by the rapid construction of these 'living and working' fortifications was Capt. Orde Charles Wingate, a young British officer posted to Palestine in 1936. A bible-thumping eccentric fired with Zionist zeal, Wingate was entrusted with the defence of the Iraqi Petroleum Company pipeline, the target of Arab guerrilla attacks. He formed a joint British-Jewish unit, known as the Special Night Squads, to combat these guerrilla forces. The HAGANAH was at first reluctant to co-operate with the British, but Wingate's sincerity and support for Zionism convinced them. He was to be seen wandering the fields of Upper Galilee alone, clutching two rifles, a bible, and a Hebrew-English dictionary.

Wingate hand-picked his men from the ranks of the NOTRIM. 'Surprise', he argued, 'was a weapon to be respected', and he trained the Jewish fighters to form mobile ambushes. British practical support for the SNS was minimal, so Wingate co-operated illegally with the HAGANAH, reinforcing his patrols

Two Jewish sergeants direct the battle at Dabburiyah, the SNS's largest military engagement in 1938. Note khaki sweater with British sergeant's chevrons, and Mauser 7.63mm pistol. (HAGANAH Archives)

with FO'SH regulars. It was a highly successful force virtually ending the Arab attacks on the pipeline. Most importantly, Wingate taught the Jewish fighters the potential of a highly trained élite; and the art of improvisation—utilising the resources available to their maximum ability.

The British viewed Wingate as a security risk and the SNS were disbanded in 1938. In 1939 the FO'SH was disbanded as well, to create a larger mobilised force known as the HI'SH (HEYL SADEH or 'Field Force'). Many believed, however, that HAGANAH and Zionist leaders had feared that FO'SH might develop into a potentially threatening autonomous élite.

The PAL'MACH

The outbreak of the Second World War found the HAGANAH supporting the British, even though the infamous 'White Paper' of 17 May 1939 halted immigration just when European Jews most desperately needed sanctuary. Although much British sympathy lay with the Arabs, they realised that the Jews were their most reliable allies in the Middle East. MI4 ran a training school (designated ME 102) for Jewish agents to be dropped into Nazi Germany, and a special relationship developed between the SOE (Special Operations Executive) and the HAGANAH. The SOE provided the fledgling HAGANAH with weapons, training, and funding while the HAGANAH provided linguistic experts and SHA'I operatives[1]. SHA'I agents and FO'SH veterans received commando training from the British for spectacular missions, which nearly included a 'scrubbed' HAGANAH sabotage raid on the Romanian oil fields at Ploesti in late 1940.

When the Allied situation in the Middle East deteriorated the HAGANAH and the British formed a special guerrilla-type force to operate behind German lines should they invade Palestine. In May 1941 the PAL'MACH (Hebrew abbreviation for 'Strike Companies') was formed under the command of Yitzhak Sadeh. The PAL'MACH's two parallel objectives were the defence of the YISHUV (the Jewish community of Palestine) from the Arabs, and defence of Palestine from Axis invasion

[1]The intelligence and counter-espionage arm of the HAGANAH, and forebear of the MOSSAD.

n the latter case the PAL'MACH was to disrupt erman lines of communication, and render enemy rfields inoperable. They were trained as guerrillas launch sharp attacks in small units; and they came expert at demolitions and intelligence-thering. Harsh commando training provided few her rewards. Recruitment was conducted in solute secrecy, and Sadeh and his subordinates refully screened each potential PAL'MACHNIK. The itish happily refrained from incorporating the L'MACH into the British Army, and in exchange L'MACH personnel files remained in HAGANAH ssession. Just two weeks after its inception, the L'MACH went into action against the Vichy rench in Lebanon and Syria.

A hundred PAL'MACH fighters, mainly from the ite 'Arab Platoon' or SHACHAR, infiltrated various wns in Lebanon and Syria, where they assisted ee French agents in covert operations. SHACHAR's mbined intelligence skills and behind-the-lines ncept of military action personified the élite status the PAL'MACH. British officers were so impressed ith the men and women of SHACHAR that officers re quoted as saying that 'every man equals a ttalion'. At about this time, British Maj. Anthony lmer set out in a small boat, the *Sea Lion*, with 23 L'MACH demolitions experts to destroy the oil fineries at Tripoli. The boat disappeared without ace, with all hands lost. The loss of 'the 23' was a rious blow for the PAL'MACH; nevertheless, ilitary operations continued.

The PAL'MACHNIKs proved to be excellent scouts, ting as guides to the advancing Allied forces in ria—among them Moshe Dayan, who lost an eye ttling the Vichy French. When Yigal Allon and a L'MACH patrol captured a bridge spanning the tani River and four POWs, a colonel from the ustralian 7th Division promised to recommend e PAL'MACHNIKs for decorations: Allon politely clined, asking instead to be allowed to keep the isoners' captured weapons. The colonel not only reed, but offered Allon a larger pile of arms ptured from the French. They were used a few ars later against the British.

By 1943, the PAL'MACH boasted over 1,000 hters. It even had a naval service, the PAL'YAM ea Companies') with courses in naval sabotage, phibious landing, naval transport, and deep-sea erations; and an air service, the PAL'AVIR ('Air

A squad from the PAL'MACH's HAREL Brigade engage the Arab Legion near Jerusalem, July 1948. The sniper fires a Lee Enfield Mk.IV fitted with sniper-scope. Note US ammunition pouches and British paratroop helmet. (IDF Archives)

Companies') with pilots trained in gliders and light transports. A PAL'MACH 'German Platoon' (or 'Middle East Commando') was formed from German and Austrian Jews who were trained as German soldiers, proficient in all types of Wehrmacht weaponry. Had the Germans reached Palestine, they would have formed a 'fifth column'; in the event they were used as intelligence agents to infiltrate POW camps. Thirty-two male and female parachutists were trained to jump into central Europe to instigate Jewish resistance: most, like the heroine Hanah Szenesh, were captured, tortured and executed. Co-operation was temporary, however: on VE Day, the PAL'MACH mobilised its forces against the British.

The PAL'MACH was the HAGANAH's field laboratory, where new systems of training and operation were tested. Most important to the PAL'MACH was the principle of leadership: officers treated their men as brothers in arms, leading by example, not privilege. The PAL'MACH 'manual' was imagination and improvisation; and although the PAL'MACHNIK was trained to fight in company and even battalion strengths, the ultimate PAL'MACH unit remained one soldier and his rifle.

When the PAL'MACH sprang into action against the British in spectacular fashion in late 1945, it took great care to attack military targets only. This policy was based on the sacred HAGANAH and later IDF principle of TOHAR HANESHEK or 'purity of arms'. Most of the PAL'MACH's operations in 1945–47 took the form of assistance to illegal immigrants breaking through the British blockade. Protesting against the blockade, the PAL'MACH attacked all 11 supposedly heavily guarded bridges leading into Palestine on the night of 17–18 June 1946, destroying ten of them. On 10 October 1946, 250 PAL'MACH commandos attacked the detention camp at Atlit, freeing scores of prisoners. It should be stressed that PAL'MACH military co-operation with the IRGUN and LEHI terror factions was minimal; the PAL'MACH even captured 'wanted' fighters from these factions, and turned them over to the British CID.

After Independence

When the UN partitioned Palestine into Jewish and Arab states, the true war for Israel's existence began. Arab bands immediately attacked Jewish settlements, while the British (who maintained a 100,000-man garrison in Palestine) confiscated HAGANAH weapons. The PAL'MACH, the HAGANAH's

Firing a jeep-mounted Boys .55 anti-tank rifle, a SHU'ALEI SHIMSHON crew engage Egyptian armour in the Negev Desert during Operation 'Ten Plagues', October 1948. The three arrows marking on the jeep is particular to IDF Southern Command. (IDF Archives)

only mobilised force, found itself engaged in fu scale war, greatly outnumbered and with the bar minimum of arms. By the end of 1947, the HAGAN armoury consisted of only 10,073 rifles, 1,9 machine guns, 440 light machine guns, and 7 mortars to defend the 600,000-strong YISHUV.

The Israel Defense Forces (TZAVA HAGAN L'YISRAEL, or 'TZAHAL') were created on 31 M 1948, consisting of eight brigades. Complementi this force were three PAL'MACH brigades command by Yigal Allon and divided along territorial zones operation: YIFTACH Bde.—three battalions oper ing in eastern Galilee; HAREL Bde.—three battalic operating in the Jerusalem area; and HANEG Bde.—four battalions, including the élite je battalion 'Negev Beasts', and an HQ battali which controlled all naval, air, and comman companies. There were also 500 women fighters full-time PAL'MACH service, who fought on all from with great courage, skill, and distinction.

Throughout the War of Independence t PAL'MACH provided the spearhead of Israel's fore in battle. The YIFTACH Bde. was instrumental in t capture of Safed from the seasoned regulars Fawzi al-Kaukji's 'Arab Liberation Army' af savage fighting. In and around Jerusalem t

ing by his 'sandwich' armoured car on the 'Burma Road'
ards Jerusalem, a PAL'MACHNIK from the PORTZIM Battalion
plays typical PAL'MACH kit, including tan-khaki fatigues,
ab *kefiyeh* worn as a scarf, woollen 'cap comforter', and
ch K98 7.92mm Mauser rifle. (HAGANAH Archives)

REL Bde., commanded by Yitzhak Rabin,[1] faced
: soldiers of Abd al-Kader al-Husseini and the
ab Legion; this region provided the site of the
aviest fighting of the war, at Kastel overlooking
: Jerusalem road. In both these actions, the
hting was restricted to close-quarter combat,
th no room to demonstrate the PAL'MACH's special
ents. It was in the Negev Desert that the
L'MACH was able to prove its élite military
tential. In the campaign in the south against the
ab Legion and the Egyptian Army, the HANEGEV
e. mounted swift attacks by 'commandos' in jeeps
ed with MG34 light machine guns and PIAT
ti-tank weapons. These units, most notably the
egev Beasts', disrupted enemy communications

with lightning raids, and assisted conventional
HAGANAH and IDF attacks with reconnaissance and
intelligence-gathering missions. Also operating in
the area was the GIVA'ATI Infantry Brigade's élite
54th Reconnaissance Battalion, known as 'Samson's
Foxes'. This unit, equipped with jeeps and M3 half-
tracks took Britain's wartime Long Range Desert
Group as its model; and, together with the HANEGEV
Bde., captured Beersheba and El-Arish, and
actually founded the city of Eilat on the Red Sea in
a race against the cease-fire clock.

The Paratroops

From 'Unit 101' to the Mitla Pass

Although the PAL'MACH had been an intrinsic
element in Israel's struggle for independence, it was
disbanded in 1949 to prevent it from becoming a
politically potent military élite. The military need
for special units remained obvious, however; and in
that same year 'Major' Yoel Palgi,[1] one of the 32
British-trained parachutists who had jumped into
central Europe, was summoned to form a
'paratroop commando' unit.

The first paratroop force was made up of those
who had jumped with the British in the Second
World War, graduates of the HAGANAH paratroop
course in Czechoslovakia, and ex-PAL'MACHNIKS.
Their beginning was shaky, at best; no training
facilities existed, and discipline was so lax that
morning roll-call was a rare event! Luckily the
fledgling paratroopers received some outstanding
volunteers, whose leadership and example forged
the unit into a cohesive military force. Notable
among these recruits were Karl Kahana, an
Austrian veteran of the LRDG, and Marcel Tuvias,
ex-French Foreign Legion. Kahana was the
professional who refined the Unit, while Tuvias,
'the endorser', battered those failing to 'fall into
line'. This unique combination, together with new
commander Maj. Yehudah Harari, (ex-IRGUN, and
former Jewish Brigade officer) made the paratroops
into a potential fighting élite.

To increase the quality of his soldiers, Harari
literally 'kidnapped' men from other units. Training fatalities lowered morale to dangerous levels,

---

e of the five PAL'MACH commanders to become IDF Chiefs of Staff:
zhak Rabin, Haim Bar-Lev, David Elazar, Mordechai Gur, Rafael
n.

[2]Palgi had been captured by the Gestapo, tortured, and escaped certain
death by jumping off the train to the gas chambers.

however, and many paratroopers demand transfers. Nevertheless, by 1950 the first 'behind t lines' jump exercise was conducted with impressi results. In 1952 the unsafe C-46 transport w replaced by some C-47 Dakotas; new parachut arrived—as did new, highly motivated recru selected for their high IQs, athletic abilities, a mental stability. Of the group of 70 'volunteer reaching the paratroops in 1953, only one was native born Israeli; the paratroops became 'Tower of Babel', where over 40 languages we spoken, and it took the relentless efforts of Hara and his deputy Capt. Aharon Davidi to forge t TZANHANIM into a capable unit. It was, howev untested in combat; and in 1953 it was unable meet Israel's immediate security threat—Ara infiltrators.

In August 1951 the IDF General Staff decided form an élite unit to secure Israel's frontiers, whi then had a certain 'Wild West' flavour. Known

Sami Rafael (right) shakes the hand of Yeshayahu Dar, whom he had just saved when his 'chute caught up on a C-46's tail. Sami wears British battledress, adorned with a light red instructor's lanyard, early cloth parachutist wings worn above left breast pocket, and yellow scarf. The HEYL RAGLIM (infantry) beret badge is worn on the dark maroon paratroop beret. (IDF Archives)

The paratroops' second and most influential command Maj. Yehuda Harari (centre, standing with beret) poses w the graduates of the IDF's first jump instructors' course, 19 The jump instructors wear British X-Type parachutes, a paratroop helmets adorned with white stencilled parachu wings. Harari wears a maroon beret with TZAHAL beret bad (IDF Archives)

Paratroop officers discuss the successful completion of Operation 'ELKAYAM', 30 August 1955. Note Australian-style 'slouch hat' and Kibbutz 'KOVA TEMBEL' ('fool's cap'); and '37-type and indigenous pouches carrying ammunition for the UZI 9mm SMG. (IDF Archives)

890th Paratroop Battalion officers pose with Chief of Staff Lt.Gen. Moshe Dayan and OC Southern Command Maj.Gen. Asaf Simchoni following Operation 'EGED', November 1955. *Standing left to right*: Lt. Meir Har-Zion, Maj. 'Arik' Sharon, Lt.Gen. Dayan, Capt. Dani Matt, Lt. Moshe Efron, and Maj.Gen. Asaf Simchoni. *Kneeling, left to right*: Capt. Aharon Davidi, Lt. Ya'akov Ya'akov, and Capt. 'Raful' Eitan. (IDF Archives)

Unit 30', it consisted of conscript 'volunteers' together with Bedouin and Circassian scouts; its task was to seek out and engage Arab infiltrators, mainly in the southern part of Israel. 'Unit 30' was small, never exceeding the strength of two platoons; it nevertheless managed to make a name for itself. Its fighters were masters of camouflage and long-range reconnaissance. The IDF of those days had done no planning on how to integrate 'special forces' on a long term basis, however, and 'Unit 30' was disbanded in 1952.

Between 1949 and 1953 the IDF increased in size, though not in quality. It was still in a period of development, and found itself ill-prepared to meet the challenge posed by the infiltrators: between 1949 and 1952 there were over 3,000 such incidents. The IDF responded by creating a small commando force, to give a lead which other units could follow. The unit was not meant to be a large conventional force, but a 'partisan' group able to cross the frontiers undetected and carry out harsh reprisals. In August 1953 a 24-year-old reserve major was summoned back to active duty: his name was Ariel 'Arik' Sharon—and the IDF's infamous 'Unit 101' was born.

Unit 101

Sharon was given a free hand to recruit his men, mainly from among those dissatisfied with the routine of 'spit and polish' military service. They flocked to Sharon, whose informality typified the unit's aura of daring and independence. The men were encouraged to be original and to use their initiative. They wore what they pleased, and carried a wide assortment of weaponry including the 'Tommy-gun', MP-40, and Molotov cocktail'. Unit 101's most famous soldier was Meir Har-Zion, a NA'HA'L reconnaissance scout with extraordinary combat and navigational skills.

There was no saluting at Camp 'STAPH', the home of this secretive unit, and relations between commander and soldiers were informal. The golden rule was that 'no one returned to base unless the mission was carried out'. The men trained constantly, utilising everything from beer bottles to overhead pigeons as targets; and explosions were heard around the clock. After two months of collective training, Unit 101's 40 men craved battle, and squads were despatched on cross-border raids. On missions, the men usually wore civilian clothing, carried no radio, had no doctor; such conditions created the unique leadership cadre associated with Unit 101—like the PAL'MACH before them, personified by the battle cry 'Follow Me!' Sharon celebrated each squad's return from a mission with a feast of delicacies.

Unit 101 conducted dozens of daring raids against Egyptian and Jordanian targets. On 13

October 1953 two Israeli children were brutally murdered by Arab infiltrators. The Jordanian village of Kibya, an Arab Legion outpost, was selected for a reprisal. It would be Unit 101's most notorious raid.

Joining Unit 101 in Operation 'SHOSHANA' was a paratroop force led by Capt. Davidi. Sharon commanded the operation, with Lt. Har-Zion commanding the covering forces lying in ambush. After successfully crossing into Jordanian territory, the attack force was spotted and a pitched battle ensued. Firing wildly, 'Kibya Task Force' commander Shlomo Baum (who carried 18 hand grenades, two 'Molotov cocktails', and ten Thompson magazines in his belt) led Davidi's force through Kibya's defences using 'Bangalore torpedoes', under intense Arab Legion fire. Sharon ordered Kibya's homes to be demolished. Paratroop sappers ordered the residents to flee, and dozens of homes were dynamited. It was later clear that not all the civilians were evacuated, as no less than 69 bodies were found in the rubble.

890th Paratroop Battalion

The Israeli government falsely denied 'official involvement' in the raid, claiming that it was the work of outraged civilians seeking revenge. Unit 101 continued its operations, but was disbanded in January 1954, and incorporated with the paratroopers, forming the 890th Paratroop Battalion. Sharon was appointed battalion commander over Yehuda Harari (causing Harari's resignation, and mass defections by loyal TZANHANIM) and hoped to attract many Unit 101 veterans to the unit. Although it had existed for only five months, the importance of Unit 101 was best summarised by Chief of Staff Moshe Dayan's speech to the fighters on the unit's final operational day: 'Maybe you *are* the chosen—but it is your responsibility to join the paratroopers and show *them* what the IDF is!'

The merger of Unit 101 and the paratroopers meant the formation of a battalion organised for large-scale operations, not just reconnaissance patrols and reprisals. The 890th Bn. sought out new and innovative commanders, mainly from the ranks of the NA'HA'L (Hebrew acronym for 'Pioneer Fighting Youth'), whose 88th Bn. was now incorporated into the paratroop force. Sharon and Davidi (who now commanded the 890th Bn.'s

Two paratroopers from the NA'HA'L 88th Bn. seen duri? Operation 'SHOMRON', the raid on Kilkilya, 10 October 19?? Tan-khaki fatigues are worn, as are British and Fren? helmets. The paratrooper on the left carries an UZI SMG wit? wooden stock, while his comrade carries the Czech K98 wi? rifle grenade firing attachment. (IDF Archives)

reconnaissance company) trained the paratroope? in the art of commando raids, as well conventional combat.

In 1955–56 the paratroopers carried out ni? major retaliatory raids. In each operation ne? weapons and tactics were utilised, as in Operatio? 'ELKAYAM', the raid on the Egyptian police statio? in Khan Yunis on 30 August 1955. Here t? battalion deployed for the first time as a mechanise? force, utilising heavily armed M3 half-tracks; and heavy fighting, 72 Egyptians were killed. ? Operation 'A'ALI ZAIT', the paratroopers used sm? rubber craft, crossing the Sea of Galilee to atta? Syrian fortifications. A reconnaissance company l? by Meir Har-Zion separated from the main for? and proceeded to kidnap two Syrian officers wh? were traded later for four Israeli POWs. Lt. Ha? Zion was awarded the OT HAOZ bravery decorati? for his courage under fire; he was critical? wounded, and released from active duty ni? months later.

The largest such operation, however, was Operation 'SHOMRON', the paratroop raid on the Kilkilya Police Station in Jordan on 10 October 1956. By 1956 the original 890th Bn. had evolved into a brigade-size force known as Unit 202. This comprised the 890th Bn. (now commanded by Maj. Rafael 'Raful' Eitan, an ex-PAL'MACHNIK and OT HA'OZ recipient), the NA'HA'L 88th Bn., and a new reserve battalion, the 771st. Operation 'SHOMRON' saw the brigade operating together for the first time, as well as being the first retaliatory paratroop raid receiving armoured and air support. A fierce battle developed in and around the Jordanian police fort; the paratroopers were newly issued with UZI SMGs. The 890th Bn. was responsible for destroying the fort, while the 88th Bn. was to provide covering force and lay ambushes for Jordanian reinforcements. The mission was carried out as planned, though with too many casualties: 18 paratroopers were killed—including Yirmi Bardanov, the battalion demolitions officer, who had been released from active service days earlier but re-joined the attack force on his own accord.

The Sinai Campaign, 1956

Just 19 days after Operation 'SHOMRON', the men of the 890th Bn. found themselves airborne over the Sinai in 16 Dakotas. At 16:59 hours on 29 October 1956 the paratroopers 'hooked up' and waited for the green light to blink. 'Raful' Eitan jumped first, followed by 350 others, landing at 'Parker Memorial', 4km west of the Mitla Pass. They were 200km from the Israeli border, 70km from the Suez Canal, and awaiting the arrival of the remainder of Unit 202. Operation 'KADESH', Israel's invasion of the Sinai Peninsula, was under way.

The paratroops were originally intended to jump over El-Arish, but the strategic Mitla Pass was eventually chosen, since intelligence and aerial photographs indicated only minor Egyptian troop activity in the area. Their mission was to pre-position an ambush force, prepared to defeat Egyptian armour and infantry reinforcements moving east into the desert to confront the IDF advance. Throughout the night of 29/30 October heavy weapons and supplies were para-dropped to the 890th Bn. The paratroopers dug in; but Eitan, becoming edgy as he waited for the Egyptians to attack, sent a patrol to the eastern opening of the

Maj. Shlomoh Baum (*left*) orders his paratroops out of the Kilkilya Police Station just prior to its demolition. Baum wears standard issue olive fatigues, and a rare short type of khaki canvas UZI ammunition pouches. Note British bayonet tucked into pistol belt. (IDF Archives)

Mitla Pass. The patrol reported heavy concentrations of Egyptian forces in ambush position; and Eitan decided to wait for Sharon, who arrived with Unit 202's other battalions at 22:30 hours.

Jealous of Eitan's battalion for jumping at Mitla, Mordechai Gur pleaded with Sharon to allow his 88th Bn. to break through the Mitla Pass. Sharon agreed, and requested permission from IDF Southern Command to authorise a 'small reconnaissance force' to enter the pass. The paratroop operation at Mitla was already causing edginess in Southern Command HQ: many felt that the paratroopers were in above their heads. Nevertheless, Sharon received authorisation for the 'reconnaissance', and proceeded to send in the entire 88th Bn., arguing that 'paratroopers go on patrols as if heading out to a major battle'; and indeed they were.

Eitan's men were bitter that the 88th Bn. were afforded the opportunity to lead the advance through Mitla: they had been the first to jump, and now the 'glory' would go to another unit. Leading the 88th Bn. column was the reconnaissance M3 half-track commanded by Lt. Arik Caspi. As Caspi reached the pass entrance he observed armed soldiers, but could not positively identify them. The battalion approached closer, and soon found itself the target of an Egyptian ambush and in a murderous cross-fire. The battle for Mitla developed into a rescue operation, with unit after unit pinned down as they were drawn into the Egyptian trap. During what developed into a desperate battle, Sharon remained at 'Parker Memorial'. Many criticised him for cowardice in not directing the rescue operation personally, though Gur was also blamed for dragging an entire battalion to possible destruction.

As the battle raged, Gur's radio communications became less coherent. Micha Kapusta's reconnaissance unit suffered heavy casualties while trying in vain to reach Gur, as Egyptian Meteors staged a strafing run. As darkness fell the fatigued paratroopers inched their way towards the mouths of the caves sheltering the Egyptians, and proceeded to

A paratroop medic from the 890th Bn. stands by the C-47 whi will ferry him to Mitla, 29 October 1956. He wears oli fatigues, an Israeli copy of a French parachute, US Arr medic's pouch, US M-1 helmet, and carries the UZI SM (IGPO)

A patrol from SAYERET SHAKED pursue Egyptian Military Intelligence agents just prior to the outbreak of the 1956 War. They wear khaki fatigues, and are lightly equipped for mobility in the desert. Note cap and US map case of officer peering through field glasses. (IDF Archives)

lob in grenade after grenade, followed by magazin loads of UZI SMG fire. One by one the Egyptia positions fell; and by midnight on 31 October t Mitla Pass was in Israeli hands. The Egyptians lo 260 killed; Unit 202 suffered 38 dead, and 1 wounded.

Although the débâcle at Mitla resulted from po communications and over-zealousness, all ran distinguished themselves in combat. Most notat of these were Oved Ledijnsky (who was killed in t battle) and Levi Hofesh, company commande who were instrumental in leading assaults agair the Egyptian firing positions in Mitla's countle 'sepulchres'. In a token military gesture on November, the 88th Bn. was parachuted into t A'tur airfield, to secure the Israeli advance Sharm es-Sheikh and the Straits of Tiran. T paratroopers returned to Israel as heroes, victors a fierce, though somewhat pointless battle.

In 1957 the paratroopers settled into a routine training and expansion. The heroic tales of Mi attracted the cream of Israel's youth; and Unit 2

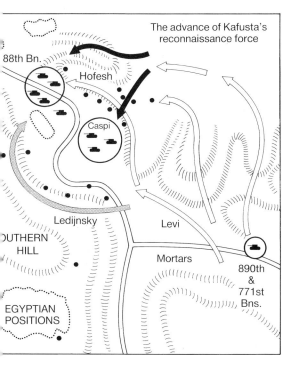

The advance of Kafusta's reconnaissance force

88th Bn.

Hofesh

Caspi

Ledijnsky

Levi

SOUTHERN HILL

Mortars

890th & 771st Bns.

EGYPTIAN POSITIONS

battle for the Mitla Pass, 31 October 1956.

…ful' Eitan's men dig in near the 'Parker Memorial', …paring firing positions for the expected Egyptian response …ch never materialised. Note BESA light machine gun, just …ble in the rear. (IDF Archives)

became HATIVAT HATZANHANIM (the Paratroop Brigade). SAYERET TZANHANIM, 'paratroop recon', was expanded into a battalion—training on enemy territory, and taking part in most of the intelligence-gathering operations of the period[1]. More than shock troops, SAYERET TZANHANIM proved to be strategic innovators, developing assault tactics with heavily armed jeeps, blazing desert trails and becoming the first IDF unit to deploy from helicopters in 1960. In 1963 HA'AN TZANHANIM (Paratroop Engineering Unit) was established, as were two reserve paratroop brigades, the 55th and 80th. The TZANHANIM acquired Nordatlas transports from France, and trained paratroop officers the world over.

In 1964, a new battalion, the 202nd, joined the brigade. Col. Eitan was appointed brigade commander, and large-scale exercises were held. From 1965 to 1967 the paratroops once again found themselves operating as a retaliatory force against guerrilla targets in Jordan and Lebanon. Four major raids were carried out, most notably

[1]On 6 September 1959, the unit's commander, Capt. Yair Peled, was brutally murdered by Bedouins during one such operation.

Operation 'MAGRESA'—the brigade-size daylight raid on the Jordanian village and guerrilla stronghold of Samua, resulting in the deaths of 19 Jordanian officers.

The 1967 Six Day War

Early on the morning of 5 June 1967, Israeli Air Force planes attacked airfields and ground targets in Egypt. Ground forces, which had been on full alert for three weeks, prepared for their pre-designated assignments. In the southern sector the mission assigned to HATIVAT HATZANHANIM was to 'purify' the enemy positions at Rafah. 'Raful's' force consisted of two paratroop battalions, an M-48 tank unit and SAYERET TZANHANIM commanded by Maj. Dan Shomron (at the time of writing the IDF Chief of Staff). At 08:55 hours dozens of M3 half-tracks ferried the paratroops across the Egyptian frontier towards Rafah; while at 18:50 hours, the 80th Reserve Para Bde. commanded by Col. Dani Matt neutralised the Egyptian artillery positions at Um Katef in a heliborne assault.

The fortifications at Rafah were stubbornly

defended, but after a day's combat resistance th Egyptians fled their positions. 'Raful' urged his me on, intending the paratroops to be the first Israe soldiers to reach the Suez Canal. Just 25km from th Canal, 'Raful' took a bullet in the head; and Co Aharon Davidi, the IDF's first KA'TZ'HA'R (Chi Paratroop and Infantry Officer), assumed com mand of HATIVAT HATZANHANIM. Days later hospital, 'Raful' received word that the paratroo had beaten the 7th Armd.Bde. to the Canal.

The paratroops' epic action of the war was th 55th Reserve Para Bde.'s assault on Jerusaler Commanded by Col. Mordechai Gur, the brigac was originally to parachute into El-Arish on 5 Jun but when Jordan commenced hostilities in Je usalem, the opportunity to 'liberate' the City David was at hand. The Jordanians, however, we determined to defend the holy city at all costs.

Ammunition Hill and the Police School we crucial positions overlooking axes of advance in Jerusalem from the north and east. Ammunitic Hill (or 'the monster') was heavily fortified, with bunkers and a series of interlocking trenches. Th Police School was also well defended, with hear machine guns and snipers; its capture was assigne to the 66th Bn.'s ALEPH Co. The Jordanians thre everything they had at ALEPH Co., including tan 25 pdr. and machine gun fire. Undaunted, t paratroops continued their advance, breaki through the outer perimeter barbed wire wi 'Bangalore torpedoes'. Once inside, the force sp into squads of four, and cleared the rooms Jordanian defenders by tossing in grenad followed by bursts of 9mm fire from their UZIs. dawn ALEPH Co. joined the battalion's assault Ammunition Hill.

By 03:40 hours, the exhausting fight for the h was under way. The Jordanians defended the positions tenaciously, turning the capture of ea bunker and trench into a major battle. T confined trenches slowed the paratroops' advan to a crawl, and many discarded their bulky pac and 'long' FNs and MAGs. In many cases, captur M-1 carbines were used as clubs in the dozens private hand-to-hand battles on the hill. Wh 'KOACH NIR', a company-size force, found its dangerously pinned down near the large 'obs vation bunker', Pte. Eitan Nava was despatched a 'suicide charge' to divert Jordanian fire aw

Paratroopers from the 88th Bn. question a Bedouin near A'tur, 3 November 1956. Note interesting olive drab para-smocks, clearly modelled on British and French types; olive fatigue trousers with large cargo pockets; brown paratroop boots; UZIs, and tan-khaki canvas grenade pouches worn by paratroopers on right. (IDF Archives)

m the company. Moments later, he was dead,[1]
t his lone gesture had restored momentum to the
ttered reservists. At 05:15 hours, the Israeli flag
is hoisted atop Ammunition Hill.

At dusk on 6 June the 71st Bn., supported by a
k company and the brigade's reconnaissance
ce (commanded by Micha Kapusta of Mitla
ne), attacked the fortifications near the Rockefel-
Museum, and secured the north-east route of
vance into the Old City. The Jordanians had
ced a strong sniper force along the Old City
lls, and the reconnaissance forces met with heavy
e. At 08:30 hours on 7 June, Gur received
thorisation to enter the Old City: the 66th Bn.
acked from Mt. Scopus, the 28th Bn. through
rod's Gate, and Kapusta's reconnaissance unit
ough the Lion's Gate—the only gate wide
ough to allow the movement of armoured
icles. At 10:00 hours, Gur addressed his officers,
nouncing: '*To all paratroop commanders: we are
ering the Old City. We will ascend to the Western
all and the Temple Mount. The Jewish Nation awaits
victory. Israel awaits this moment in history. Ascend and
ieve victory!*' Through the narrow alleyways of the
(market) in the Arab quarter, the men gingerly
ceeded towards the Wailing Wall, the holiest site
Judaism. An hour later, Gur's voice once again
errupted the communication network, proclaim-
'*The Temple Mount is in our hands—I repeat—the
mple Mount is in our hands!*' Jerusalem was unified
last.

Although a major heliborne operation by Col.
tt's 80th Bde. was conducted to secure the
thern Golan Heights on 9 June, the 'liberation'
Jerusalem was a victory of greater political and
igious significance. A special bond developed
ween the city and the paratroopers, and all
atroop and élite forces swearing-in ceremonies
e since taken place at the Wailing Wall.

e War of Attrition and after, 1967–73: e Jordan Valley

rge scale Palestinian guerrilla infiltration across
Jordan River began immediately following the
Day War. The mountainous desert region of the
dan Valley was ideal for guerrilla activity,
ering sanctuary in thousands of uncharted caves

his courage, Pte. Nava was posthumously awarded Israel's highest
al for bravery, the OT HAGVURA—'Order of Courage'.

and ravines; and 'Raful', fully recovered from his
head wound, was charged with establishing law and
order in the area. Realizing that a non-
conventional approach was needed, he formed
HATIVAT HA'BIKA'A ('Valley Brigade') from paratroop and élite infantry formations, hand picking
his commanders, including veteran paratroopers
such as deputy brigade commander Lt. Col. Arik
Regev, and the brigade's brilliant young operations
officer, Lt. Gad Manela.

The campaign in the Jordan Valley became
known as the MIRDAFIM or 'pursuits'. Once
informed that the border had been crossed, a force
of anything from platoon to battalion size would
initiate a pursuit on foot and by helicopter, ceasing
only when the guerrillas were killed or captured.
Cross-border ambushes were also carried out by
small bands of paratroops, heli-lifted to points of

Paratroops undergo 'balancing manoeuvres', 1959. Note
explosives in tan-khaki pack secured by rope to an infantry
packboard. He wears the three-pocket olive fatigue trousers
and brown leather paratroop boots. (IDF Archives)

A SEREN (captain) of SAYERET GOLANI, (centre) directs platoon-level manoeuvres near the Syrian border, March 1964. He wears French airborne issue 'lizard-pattern' camouflage fatigues; his two deputies wear olive fatigues with olive indigenous so-called 'Battledress' spring jackets, later dubbed 'Bar-Lev' jackets, with dark green fur collars. Note captured Czech Vz-25 9mm SMG carried; this was supplied to Syria in great numbers. (IDF Archives)

access across the Jordan River. The success of the 'pursuit' depended on many crucial elements, including speed, communications, and firepower: most important, however, was leadership. 'Raful' realized that the lengthy operations in hostile and unfamiliar territory would unnerve the young conscripts, and ordered senior officers to lead each MIRDAF. This instilled confidence in the ranks, though resulting in the combat fatalities of many of HATIVAT HA'BIKA'A's commanding officers, including Regev and Manela, killed on 26 July 1968 during a routine pursuit which cornered eight guerrillas at a cave. Lt.Col. Regev (then HATIVAT HA'BIKA'A's commander) led the assault, and was killed immediately by a burst of AK-47 fire. Manela instinctively went in after the killers of his beloved commander, and he, too, was felled with a burst of automatic fire from inside the cave. (An agricultural co-operative, MOSHAV ARGAMAN, from the combined names of both Arik Regev and Gad Manela, was founded near the spot where the two had been killed.)

Newly commissioned paratroop and GOLANI officers (note soldier in background with peaked officer's cap and infantry beret badge) stand at attention at BA'HAD I, the IDF's Officers' Academy. The paratroop SEGEN (first lieutenant), wears the olive YARKIT four-pocket paratroop Class A blouse, Class A olive trousers, brown boots, and red beret. Silver metal parachutist wings (KNAFEI TZNICHA) are worn above the left breast pocket with blue background; the SIKAT ME'MEM, or officer's qualification pin, is worn on the left collar. Note khaki canvas pistol belt, supporting a holster (hidden from view). (IDF Archives)

The MIRDAFIM were the by-products of the we entrenched Palestinian guerrilla infrastructure Jordan. On 21 March 1968 the IDF raided t town of Karameh (a major guerrilla staging are in Operation 'TOFET'. HATIVAT HATZANHANI commanded by Col. Dani Matt, and an armour element from the élite 7th Armd.Bde. crossed t Jordan River on hastily constructed Bailey bridg while SAYERET TZANHANIM, commanded by M. Matan Vilnai, was heli-lifted to Karameh's easte road junction. The main force commanded by Ma engaged both Palestinian guerrillas and Jordani Army regulars in fierce fighting. Tank and a battles ensued; and following the day-long batt the IDF withdrew, suffering 28 dead. T Palestinians chose to regard Karameh as a victor although 61 Jordanians and 150 Palestinian fight were killed, with a further 128 taken prisoner.

The 1970 Jordanian civil war[1] virtually stopp

[1]See MAA 194, *Arab Armies of the Middle East Wars* (2).

filtration into Israel, except by those escaping the wrath of King Hussein's Bedouin soldiers. A state of semi-tranquillity settled over the border, which continues today, a testament to the paratroops who fought there, and to the paratroops who now patrol the same desert wilderness.

The Egyptian Front

Three weeks after the Six Day War, Egyptian artillery and commando attacks began against Israeli positions along the Suez Canal. The IDF responded with aerial and artillery bombardments of their own; and paratroops were despatched to stabilise the area. Lengthy patrols were initiated against marauding Egyptian commandos, and the paratroops secured the IDF lines of communication from enemy interference. Between November 1968 and January 1970, paratroop and recon forces conducted 12 large-scale raids against targets deep inside Egyptian territory; these ranged from lobbing mortar shells at an Egyptian naval base on the Red Sea (Operation 'Buffalo'—23/12/69), to seizing Shedwan Island for over 24 hours (Operation 'RODOS'—22/1/70). The two most famous raids, however, were Operations 'HELEM' and 'TARNEGOL 53'.

Operation 'HELEM' (1 November 1968) was the paratroops' first overt long-range raid into Egypt. The objective was the destruction of the electrical power station at Nadja'a-Hamadi in the Nile Valley, over 300km from Israel, by a heliborne commando force. The brainchild of KA'TZ'HA'R Brig.Gen. 'Raful' Eitan, the operation was carried out by SAYERET TZANHANIM's 14 best fighters, commanded by Capt. Matan Vilnai. The attack

Syria and Lebanon

In the summer of 1968, Israel faced a new secur[ity] threat: international terrorism. At first the attac[k] were directed against EL AL (Israel national airline[) and other airlines serving Israel. Since the attac[k] originated from Beirut, a spectacular act [of] retaliation was planned to 'teach the Lebanese [a] lesson'. On 28 December, under 'Raful's' dire[ct] command, three Super-Frelons and two Bell-2[06] ferried a paratroop force to Beirut Internatio[nal] Airport. While one group proceeded to block [all] movement in and out of the airport, sapp[ers] achieved the demolition of every Lebanese MI[F] airliner on the tarmac—14 in all. Not one shot w[as] fired during the entire operation, though t[he] burning airliner skeleton remained as a mark of t[he] paratroops' destructive potential.

Although the paratroops conducted numero[us] raids against Syrian and Lebanese targets (inclu[d]ing a spectacular attack on a Syrian military base [at] Sue'da in Operation 'SHEFET'—17/6/70), m[ost] commando-style operations had terrorists as the[ir] targets. The largest of these was Operation 'BARD[AS] 54-55', the amphibious and heliborne paratro[op] assault on the *el-Fatah* naval commando base nor[th] of Tripoli on the night of 20–21 February 1972. T[he] operation depended on close-knit air and naval c[o-]operation, and KA'TZ'HA'R Brig.Gen. Emman[uel] 'Mano' Shaked (an ex-PAL'MACHNIK, and de[c]orated recon paratrooper), commanded the enti[re] operation from the deck of an IDF/Navy missi[le] boat. The assault force, commanded by Col. U[zi] Yairi, landed by Zodiac craft 6km from the targ[et] following a rather nauseating journey for the 'lan[d]-loving' paratroopers. After a brisk forced marc[h] the sentries were 'taken out' with silenced UZI SMG[s] and the base was attacked. In an intelligence cou[p] entire filing cabinets were removed from t[he] buildings before the facilities were destroyed. Ov[er] 30 terrorists were killed in the raid; the paratroo[ps] and Naval Commandos suffered eight wounded[.]

(Other such operations conducted by Nav[al] Commando and SAYERET units will be discussed [in] later sections.)

The 1973 War

The War of Attrition established the paratroops [as] the IDF's principal 'commando' force; yet wh[en] Egypt and Syria simultaneously attacked Israel [on]

A SAYERET GOLANI officer directs a training exercise, January 1966. All wear 'lizard-pattern' fatigues, indigenously incorporated with a 'Battledress' jacket. Note black ELBA boots, khaki canvas web gear, and folding-stock UZI variant fitted with two clipped magazines. (IDF Archives)

force landed 5km from the target, neutralised the Egyptian defenders and destroyed the power station. The raid highlighted Egyptian vulnerability, and for two months after the raid peace came to the front.

In mid-December 1969, IAF aerial photographs revealed the establishment of an extensive Egyptian air-radar network. The General Staff ordered their 'termination', but 'Raful' had grander ambitions and presented plans for the kidnapping of a complete, operable, 15 ton Soviet P-12 radar. On 27 December, a sizeable NA'HA'L paratroop force landed at Ras Arab, and proceeded to silence all opposition and to prepare the radar for a return flight to Israel. Time was of the essence as a major Egyptian garrison was only a few miles away; and it took the paratroopers only four hours to prepare the P-12 for transport. Following this raid the paratroops' 'mission impossible' reputation passed securely into legend.

October 1973, launching the 1973 Yom Kippur
ar, the paratroops found themselves operating as
nventional mechanised infantrymen. HATIVAT
TZANHANIM (by now designated as the 35th
ra Bde., under the command of Col. Uzi Yairi)
w action on the southern front, together with the
7th Reserve Para Bde. (formerly the 55th)
mmanded by Col. Dani Matt; while the 317th
ormerly 80th) Reserve Para Bde. was mobilised
service in the Golan Heights with the NA'HA'L
th Para Battalion. Although the 1973 War is best
membered as a 'tank war', it was the paratroops,
always, who led the vanguard.

In Sinai, the 35th Bde. entered the fighting on 8
ctober, battling heliborne Egyptian commandos
ar Ras Sudr in 'pursuits' similar to those of the
rdan Valley, and lifting the Egyptian siege of the
rthernmost Bar-Lev Line fortification at
JDAPEST'. The 247th Bde. attached its battalions
the armoured brigades containing the Egyptian
islaught; and following the historic armoured
ttle of 14 October (the second largest tank battle
military history), it prepared for the most
iportant operation of the campaign: Operation
tout-Hearted'—the crossing of the Suez Canal
to Egyptian Africa.

The lead force which crossed the Canal in rubber
nghies on the night of 15/16 October consisted of
ly 36 men from the brigade's SAYERET, and the
th Bde.'s élite 'Amphibious Sapper Unit'. It was
o days before the Egyptians discovered their
idgehead, which facilitated the crossing of the
tire 247th Bde. as well as two complete armoured
visions. A fierce battle developed; though it did
it approach in scope and ferocity that which broke
it at the Chinese Farm on the east bank of the
inal.

To secure the crossing from both sides, a
ttalion from the 247th Bde. was sent to clear the
yptian-occupied Chinese Farm, a vital choke
•sition controlling the AKAVISH, LEXINCON, and
RTUR roads. The routine operation developed
to a battle of survival, as patrol after patrol of
ratroopers came under murderous Egyptian
issile and small arms fire. On 16 October the 35th
le.[1] were sent in to rescue the badly mauled

reservists, but they too found themselves fighting for
their lives. In the three-day battle the paratroops
suffered over 50 dead and hundreds of wounded.

Meanwhile, on the west bank of the Canal, the
IDF met with determined though crumbling
resistance. This led to a false sense of security in the
IDF camp; and on 24 October, the last days of
fighting before a UN-imposed cease-fire, a paratroop battalion was sent into Suez City to gain
territory. In Suez, the paratroops found themselves
in the midst of a determined Egyptian commando
force; and were forced to withdraw at nightfall after
suffering dozens of dead and wounded.

On the northern front, elements of the NA'HA'L's
50th Para Bn. heroically defended the line against
advancing Syrian armour and infantry forces, not
relinquishing a single position. There were numerous paratroop raids against Syrian targets,
including the destruction of a bridge in eastern
Syria by a heli-borne HA'AN TZANHANIM force,
though most of these operations remain highly
classified. The final mission of the 317th Bde. was
assisting the GOLANI Infantry Bde. in the recapture
of Mt. Hermon. Four CH-53 helicopters ferried the
paratroop force to the Syrian peak of Mt. Hermon;
and although the heavily armed Syrian com-

A reconnaissance paratrooper from SAYERET TZANHANIM tosses
in an anti-personnel grenade during assault exercises. He
wears general service issue French 'lizard' fatigues, and
carries the Israeli-produced FN 7.62mm squad support
weapon, the bipod wrapped with hessian for grip and
camouflage. The white tape across the helmet is for station-
keeping at night. (IDF Archives)

igade commander Yairi survived the Chinese Farm, only to be killed
) years later leading the rescue operation at Tel Aviv's Savoy Hotel,
.ed by 'Black September' terrorists on 5 March 1975.

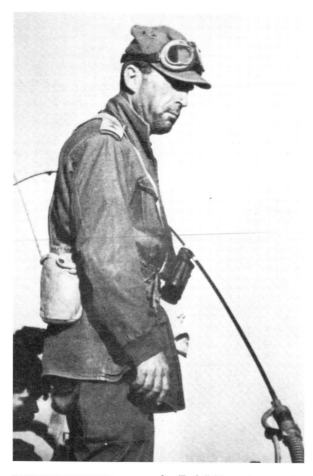

HATIVAT HATZANHANIM commander 'Raful' Eitan observes the battle at Rafah, 5 June 1967. He wears an olive field cap with khaki-bound brim, olive smock and three-pocket fatigue trousers. The three green-stencilled FALAFELs on the rank slide indicate ALUF MISHNE, colonel. (IGPO)

mandos put up a stiff resistance with heavy RPG and sniper fire, the position fell by the day's end.

The 'armoured bias' of the 1973 war introduced profound changes into the paratroops' combat doctrine. Hand-held 66mm LAW rockets and jeep and M113 mounted TOWs were incorporated in massive numbers, as the paratroops took on the IDF's anti-tank responsibility with the formation of SAYERET OREV (the paratroop reconnaissance anti-tank battalion). Terrorism, however, and not Arab tanks, remained Israel's most pressing security threat, requiring the TZANHANIM's unique talents.

Entebbe

The hijacking of Air France Flight 139 to Entebbe, Uganda, on 27 June 1976 by four PFLP terrorists at first seemed routine; but when all the hostages except for the Israelis and Jews were releas[ed] KA'TZ'HA'R Brig.Gen. Dan Shomron was summon[ed] to provide a military solution. Three plans w[ere] considered, including a brigade para-drop i[n] Entebbe itself; but in the end a quick air rescue w[as] chosen. The mission was codenamed Operati[on] 'Thunderball', and was commanded by Lt.C[ol.] Yonatan 'Yoni' Netanyahu. A full-scale model [of] the terminal housing the hostages was construct[ed] and the paratroop and recon unit selected for [the] mission trained around the clock, perfecting assa[ult] techniques in the shortest time humanly possib[le.] On 2 July a 'dry run' was conducted, including [the] 130 Hercules transports, before the pleased eyes [of] Chief of Staff Lt.Gen. Mordechai Gur.

At 16:00 hours on 3 July, four C-130s took [off] from Ophira Air Force Base loaded with the resc[ue] force; the 450-minute flight reached Entebbe o[nly] 30 seconds behind schedule. As the lead C-1[30] taxied to a halt, paratroopers jumped out at p[re-] positioned points to place emergency beacons [and] runway lights. The lead column of vehic[les] (including a black Mercedes and Land Rovers [to] impersonate President Idi Amin's entourag[e]) proceeded to eliminate two Ugandan sentries, a[nd] 15 seconds later the paratroops had begun th[e] systematic elimination of the terrorists and t[he] rescue of the 103 hostages—a task performed w[ith] split-second timing and deadly accuracy. Th[e] other C-130s landed, unloading reinforceme[nts] including a mechanised force from SAYERET GOLA[NI] and Shomron's command jeep. The entire op[er-] ation from touchdown to last lift-off took exactly [99] minutes, and resulted in the deaths of 13 terrori[sts] and 35 Ugandans, and the destruction of [11] Ugandan Air Force MiGs. Most importantly t[he] mission brought back to Israel 100 ex-hosta[ges] (three were killed in the assault), as well as the bo[dy] of the operation's commander, Lt.Col. Netanyah[u,] the sole military casualty.

Operation 'Peace For Galilee'

On 6 June 1982 the IDF, commanded by Chief [of] Staff Lt.Gen. 'Raful' Eitan, invaded Lebanon wi[th] 60,000 troops in an effort to rid her northern bord[er] of the incessant terrorist harassment. In t[he] campaign's coastal sector a large portion of the 35th Para Bde. (commanded by KA'TZ'HA'R Brig.G[en.] Amos Yaron, operations officer of the 55th Bde.

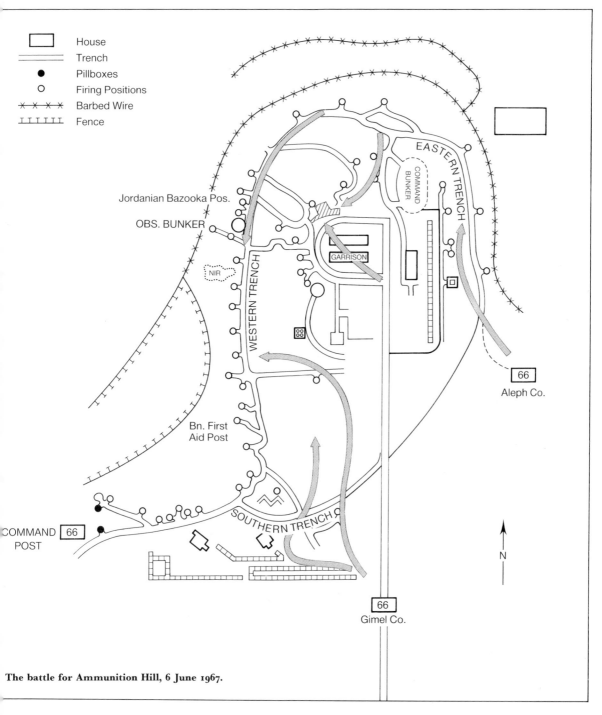

House
Trench
Pillboxes
Firing Positions
Barbed Wire
Fence

Jordanian Bazooka Pos.

OBS. BUNKER

NIR

WESTERN TRENCH

GARRISON

COMMAND BUNKER

EASTERN TRENCH

COMMAND BUNKER

66
Aleph Co.

Bn. First
Aid Post

COMMAND
POST

66

SOUTHERN TRENCH

N

66
Gimel Co.

The battle for Ammunition Hill, 6 June 1967.

67), including SAYERET TZANHANIM and the ?HA'L's 50th Para Bn., landed near the Awali ?ver on 7 June. It was the IDF's largest ever mphibious assault, and the paratroops were ?trusted with the capture of the PLO stronghold of ?on and the Ein el-Hilweh refugee camp. The ?ratroops were eager to fight on dry land following ? turbulent sea journey; but the determined

Palestinian defence would soon have disheartened the bravest of men. The costly advance through Sidon's heavily defended streets and *casbah* seasoned the paratroops for Ein el-Hilweh. Unable to utilise their heavy firepower out of concern for the civilian populace, the paratroops were forced to rely on their combat skills and unit cohesion. The camp's urban squalor provided perfect cover for the

The deputy commander of the 66th Bn. calls in artillery support during the closing stages of the fight for Ammunition Hill. Note AN/PRC-25 field radio carried on an infantry packboard; British paratroop helmets fitted with tan netting, and IDF-issue canteens. The radioman has found a practical means for carrying the radio handset, attached to his helmet chin straps. (IDF Archives)

defending Palestinians, and each alleyway, house, and room had to be fought for: the TZANHANIM suffered horrific casualties. Brig.Gen. Yaron was forced further to deplete his reserves, and heli-lift an additional battalion to Ein el-Hilweh, which was not neutralised until seven days later.

Following Ein el-Hilweh, the paratroops led the IDF advance to Beirut, where they took part in bitter fighting against Syrian commandos and PLO regulars. In the eastern sector, a special brigade-size force (KOACH PELED) had been built around SAYERET OREV to deal with Syrian armour. Equipped with M113s and jeeps mounted with TOW missiles, and foot soldiers carrying Dragons, LAWs, and RPGs, SAYERET OREV disrupted Syrian lines of communication by ambushing Syrian vehicles along the Beka'a Valley's narrow, twisting roads. In the bloody battle of Jebel Barouk they

proved their unique skills, destroying dozens T-62s, and being the only Israeli unit to destroy Syrian T-72: in fact, they achieved a greater tan kill rate than did the Israeli tank forces.

When the invasion of Lebanon developed into occupation of indeterminate length, the paratroo once again found themselves pursuing guerril and conducting retaliatory raids, against bo fanatical Shi'ites and returning Palestinian gu rillas. This period, known as 'Iron Fist', saw t formation of a new breed of paratroop soldier a officer, brutalised by the endless operations in hostile environment against a shrewd and dead enemy. Transformed into more than mere season veterans, they were forced to become bitter fighte relying on the élite nature of their training a heritage for survival.

The 35th Paratroop Brigade and its reser counterparts remain the striking edge of the Isr Defense Forces, set apart by their hard-earn legend, the parachutist wings insignia, and t motto 'After the Paratroops'.

The GOLANI Infantry Brigade

The 1st GOLANI Infantry Brigade was one of the ~~~en original HAGANAH territorial brigades, re~~onsible for the Galilee region. It enjoyed a fine ~~~mbat reputation in the War of Independence, ~~rticipating in the battles for Safed and Eilat. ~~llowing the 1948 War the IDF developed into ~~rael's 'melting pot', absorbing hundreds of ~~ousands of new immigrants from over 60 nations. ~~LANI received a disproportionate number of ~~migrants, many of whom were illiterate, un~~sciplined and unwilling to soldier. The brigade ~~ly earned a reputation as the IDF's 'trash bag', its ~~erational performance doing little to discourage ~~s negative image.

In the early 1950s the sensation surrounding Unit ~~1 and the paratroops further lowered GOLANI's ~~f-esteem, leading the General Staff to reconsider ~~e rôle of the brigade within the IDF. The ~~igade's equipment and manpower were up~~aded to 'élite status'; and junior paratroop officers ~~ere transferred into GOLANI's ranks, improving discipline, morale, and combat spirit. Intensive training routines were initiated, including the infamous GOLANI annual cross-country march from Galilee to the Gulf of Eilat. On 25 October 1955 GOLANI units joined the 890th Para Bn. in raiding an Egyptian outpost near Nitzana. Twelve months later, GOLANI played a major rôle in Operation 'KADESH', capturing the strategic Rafah crossroads.

GOLANI's true emergence as an élite fighting formation can be traced back to 1959 with the formation of SAYERET GOLANI, the brigade's reconnaissance force. Unlike other SAYEROT, SAYERET GOLANI (or the 'Flying Leopards', a reference to its recon wing insignia) did not accept conscript volunteers. Instead, its volunteers were the best GOLANI had to offer—soldiers and NCOs who had proved their combat worth. They were the only applicants allowed to qualify for the trial week or GIBUSH which tests the candidate's mental, physical and psychological limits. Those passing this ordeal undergo further examinations, and a further six months' training, the successful completion of which permits 'formal' volunteering into the SAYERET. This strict recruitment procedure made SAYERET GOLANI into one of the IDF's premier reconnaissance units.[1]

SAYERET GOLANI's training routine was brutal, and included 100km forced marches with 50kg

[1]See Sayeret Golani, *Military Illustrated Past & Present* No. 5, 1987.

~~ratroopers from the 71st Bn. take a well-deserved break ~~lowing the battle for the Rockefeller Museum. Note ~~/PRC-10s carried in tan rucksacks on infantry packboards. ~~)F Archives)

packs, as well as intensive firing exercises. SAYERET GOLANI did not accept supermen, nor did it produce them: it installed instead a deep emotional bond between soldier, commander and unit, typical of all IDF élite units, and one of the main factors behind their combat proficiency. The SAYERET set an example which the entire brigade followed closely; and within a year of its inception, the GOLANI Bde.'s five other battalions—1st 'Lightning' Bn. (G'DUD BARAK), 72nd 'First Conquerors' Bn. (HABOK'IM HARISHONIM), 17th 'Gideon' Bn. (G'DUD GIDEON), 13th Bn., and the NCOs' Course Bn. 'Golan Lions' (ARAYOT HAGOLAN)—had their first opportunity to prove their new-found combat proficiency in Operation 'HARGOL', a raid on the Syrian mortar positions at Tewfiq on 31 January 1960.

The raid on Tewfiq, brought the brigade some long overdue publicity; and in 1961 Col. Mordechai Gur left the paratroops to assume command of GOLANI. He brought with him many of the paratroops' élite traditions, and worked feverishly to develop a close bond between the command echelon and the ranks. Gur up-graded the combat status of the GOLANI even further by offering parachute training to the brigade's outstanding soldiers.

On 16 March 1962, the Syrians fired on an Israeli

A paratrooper fires his FN 7.62mm rifle at a Jordanian sniper just inside the Old City walls, 7 June 1967. (IGPO)

Police launch in the Sea of Galilee. This was the final straw in a long series of Syrian artillery attacks and Syrian artillery at the village of Nuqieb was chosen for retaliation. Although a paratroop battalion was available in the area, Chief of Staff Lt.Gen. Tzvi Tzur opted to deny himself 'the sure thing', and sent in GOLANI. The attack force was divided into five groups, with SAYERET GOLANI—commanded by Maj. Tzvika Ofer—in the van guard. A surprise attack was impossible, as the only access was a narrow stretch of lakeside road. Upon crossing the frontier, SAYERET GOLANI found itself hampered by several Syrian ambushes, but managed to extricate itself and proceed to the gun positions at Nuqieb, while the remaining GOLANI units continued on to the village itself. Fifty-three Syrian soldiers were killed that night, GOLANI suffering seven dead and 43 wounded. Operation 'SNUNIT' firmly established GOLANI's operational reign in the north, and laid the solid foundations for a combat reputation equal to that of the paratroops.

The 1967 War

Although the Six Day War began on 5 June, GOLANI received its orders to seize the Golan Heights from Syria only on 9 June. The steep cliffs were considered by many to be impassable under heavy fire, and were well defended by Syrian troops concentrated in a series of heavily fortified positions and forts.

The advance up the 1,500m-high slopes of the Golan Heights came under accurate Syrian fire. HABOK'IM HARISHONIM assaulted the fortifications at Tel A'ziziyat, seizing the position in a wide flanking attack, while BARAK was to neutralise and capture the fortifications at Tel Fahar. Tel Fahar was considered the easier target of the two, since it was a secondary position; it was, however, well entrenched, and protected by an extensive land-mine network. It consisted of two observation posts, the northern one dominating the position.

BARAK had trained long and hard for this moment, and morale was high. Battalion commander Lt.Col. Musa Klein had instilled in his unit an *esprit de corps* best characterised by the notorious story of a young rifleman brought before Klein for a disciplinary offence, whose punishment was being ordered not to take part in the assault on Tel Fahar. He cried and pleaded with Klein until the

cellent view of the equipment worn by a SAYERET SHIRION ank commander in Sinai, 9 June 1967. He wears olive tanker's veralls, a modified ex-US Army pierced crash helmet with ded communications equipment, and carries a Beretta 951S in an olive canvas holster. (IDF Archives)

A SAYERET GOLANI sergeant cocks his weapon for the cameras, January 1968. He wears a black beret with infantry beret badge on red background, olive Class A fatigues, and tan-khaki webbing. Above the left breast pocket is the 1967 campaign ribbon, the 'Flying Leopard' SAYERET GOLANI reconnaissance wings, and basic parachutist wings, both wings with green (recon) background. (IDF Spokesman)

nishment was withdrawn. In other instances, jured officers escaped hospital beds to rejoin their its.

At 13:00 hours, following a massive air and tillery barrage, the battalion advanced towards l Fahar against a hail of small arms and anti-tank e. The Syrian barrage made command and mmunications most difficult, and the extensive inefields did not allow a flanking assault. The ttalion, now forced to attack Tel Fahar by frontal sault, split into squads of 14. These advanced ong parallel paths to the outer perimeter fence, here soldiers ran over the backs of comrades who ade human bridges by dropping on the coils of rbed wire. Many of the battalion's officers were led in the attack, including Klein, felled by a iper's bullet. The leaderless men were involved in close-quarter battle to clear the trenches; where mm mortars were used at close ranges. SAYERET

GOLANI was called in, assaulting the northern observation post to end the day's long battle. GOLANI lost 22 dead at Tel Fahar.

Following Tel Fahar, the brigade continued its advance through the Golan Heights, taking the 'capital' of the Heights, Kuneitra, while the GIDEON Bn. were heli-lifted by S-58s to the southern peak of Mt. Hermon. Thirteen positions in all were captured by the GOLANI Bde. during the two days of fighting, which left 59 dead and 160 wounded.

The War of Attrition

Immediately following the 1967 War, GOLANI found itself battling Palestinian guerrillas operating against the areas of Beit Shean and the northern Jordan Valley. They initiated difficult patrols along the undefined frontiers, as well as dozens of cross-

25

A sergeant from the NA'HA'L's 50th Para Bn. *c.*1968, displays the red paratroop beret with infantry beret badge, and NA'HA'L paratroop insignia worn above the basic parachutist wings. (IDF Archives)

border ambushes. On the northern frontier, GOLANI operated daily in the campaign against the Palestinian terrorist infrastructure in southern Lebanon: laying mines, preparing ambushes, and raiding known guerrilla targets. The bitter battles between GOLANI and the guerrillas in the harsh environs of 'Fatahland' (the area around the Lebanese slopes of Mt. Hermon) have become legendary. The largest operation of the period was the raid on the guerrilla base at the Lebanese village of Ya'atur, 13km from the Israeli border, on 27 December 1970. SAYERET GOLANI elements set a desperate pace along a rocky, virtually impassable path towards the target. Addressing Ya'atur's sentries in Arabic, the assault squads quickly seized control of the base, destroying the facilities.

In 1970–71 the Gaza Strip developed into a major hotbed of terrorist activity. OC Southern Command, Maj.Gen. 'Arik' Sharon, despatched recon paratroop and SAYERET GOLANI units to liquidate the terrorists at any cost, by any mean Operating in teams of four, many times weari civilian clothing, and with fingers always on t trigger, these units sought out and destroyed t terrorists throughout Gaza.

The Yom Kippur War

The Syrian attack on the Golan Heights at 13: hours on 6 October 1973 found the GOLANI Bc dispersed and in disarray. HABOK'IM HARISHON had just returned from an extended tour of duty Gaza and was in the process of re-organisatio BARAK and SAYERET GOLANI were on holiday leav and the other units were preparing for the brigade 25th anniversary celebration in Tel Aviv. Only t GIDEON Bn. was at a high state of alert, manning t MUTZAVIM (fortifications) along the 'Purple Lin separating Israel and Syria. Thirteen GIDEC riflemen manned the ultra-sensitive Mt. Herme observation post, which was quickly seized Syrian commandos in the opening moments fighting.

The Syrian attack was massive, and t MUTZAVIM were quickly surrounded; but t GIDEON squads held on for dear life, not relinquis ing a single position. Sukhoi-7 fighter-bombe attempted to flush the defenders out, and some we shot down with .50 calibre machine gun fire; in a GOLANI shot down 17 Syrian aircraft. Some of t MUTZAVIM were defended by as few as 15 soldier though squads from SAYERET GOLANI reinforc them at later intervals. BARAK fought ne Hushniya, rescuing wounded tankers, whi HABOK'IM HARISHONIM destroyed a helibor Syrian commando force near Nafekh. Slowly t tide turned, and GOLANI joined in the counte offensive into Syria. One major task still lay ahea the recapture of the 'eyes and ears of Israel', M Hermon.

A token attempt was made on 8 October when composite company from SAYERET GOLANI led SAYERET commander Capt. Shmaryahu Vini together with forces from ARAYOT HAGOLAN ar HABOK'IM HARISHONIM, advanced up the narro mountain paths on foot and by half-track. Syri resistance was fierce, and following a relentle close-quarter fight, GOLANI retreated, suffering dead and 57 wounded.

Thirteen days later, Mt. Hermon was retaken

two-brigade assault (together with the 317th serve Para Bde.)—Operation 'KINUACH'. BOK'IM HARISHONIM put in a frontal assault, mbing through the hills leading up to the Israeli servation post, while BARAK and ARAYOT GOLAN attacked from the south-east preventing y enemy retreat. SAYERET GOLANI attacked in the nguard, racing uphill towards the upper cable position, and pinning down the Syrian nmando forces. The rocky terrain provided rfect cover for Syrian sniper teams, and every few rds advanced by GOLANI was paid for in blood. e battle for the upper cable car station was vage, and SAYERET GOLANI sustained heavy sualties in hand-to-hand combat including Capt. nik himself. (GOLANI lost many of its best officers ring the war, including the deputy brigade mmander, and the battalion commanders from : SAYERET, BARAK, and ARAYOT HAGOLAN.) At :00 hours on 21 October, the brigade flag was isted atop Mt. Hermon, and the bodies of the

brigade's 55 dead and 79 wounded were lowered down.

GOLANI paid a high price during its 18 days of combat, suffering a total of 130 dead, and 310 wounded.

GOLANI vs. Terrorism

On 15 May 1974 a school house with over 90 students in the northern border town of Ma'alot was seized by three DFLP terrorists. SAYERET GOLANI stormed the building, but the terrorists turned their weapons first on the hostages, and subsequently on themselves: 25 students were killed, a further 70 wounded. This tragedy underscored the urgent need for rescue assault tactics to be refined. Later the following month, three *el-Fatah* terrorists landed by boat and seized a block of flats

Operation 'TOFET', 3 March 1968: paratroopers engage a PFLP machine gun nest in the outskirts of Karameh, affording excellent view of tan-khaki web gear, and the positioning of the canteens, grenade and magazine pouches. Note grenadier moving into position, left. (IDF Archives)

in Nahariya. With Ma'alot still fresh in their minds, a SAYERET GOLANI squad assaulted the target with stealth and speed. The results: three dead terrorists, no civilian or GOLANI casualties. Two years later, at Entebbe, SAYERET GOLANI was committed in a support rôle, taking part in the destruction of the Ugandan MiGs. Upon their return to Israel GOLANI was finally recognised as an élite unit: its soldi᠎ discarded their despised khaki-green 'Gene᠎ Services' beret, and were issued with their o᠎ distinctive deep brown beret.

On 6 April 1980 a five-man terrorist team fr᠎ the 'Arab Liberation Front' (ALF) crossed ᠎ Lebanese border and seized the nursery at Kibb᠎

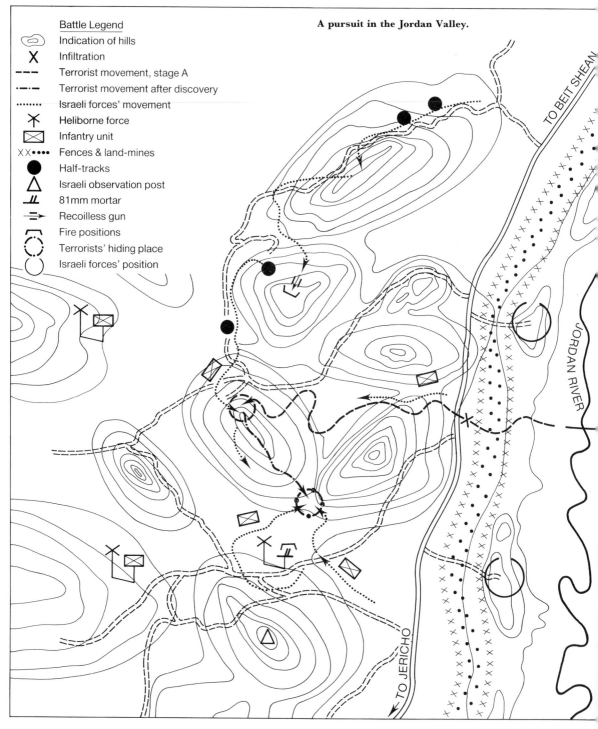

A pursuit in the Jordan Valley.

Battle Legend
- ⬭ Indication of hills
- X Infiltration
- --- Terrorist movement, stage A
- -·-· Terrorist movement after discovery
- ······· Israeli forces' movement
- ⚕ Heliborne force
- ⊠ Infantry unit
- X X ···· Fences & land-mines
- ● Half-tracks
- △ Israeli observation post
- ⊥ 81mm mortar
- ⇒ Recoilless gun
- ⌐ Fire positions
- (⌐) Terrorists' hiding place
- (Israeli forces' position

TO BEIT SHEAN

JORDAN RIVER

TO JERICHO

sgav Am. The first attempt by SAYERET GOLANI
storm the building failed, as the heavily armed
rorists (even firing RPGs) stood fast, killing one
on infantryman—and a sleeping child for good
asure. The second attempt succeeded but the
raged SAYERET vowed revenge.

Ten months after the ordeal at Misgav Am, on 22
bruary 1981, a force consisting of SAYERET
LANI's best officers and NCOs, commanded by
brigade commander, landed by helicopter 5 km
m the southern Lebanese village of El-Kfur,
dquarters of the ALF. Force A, under the
mmand of SAYERET GOLANI commander Capt.
ni Harnik set out on foot to blow up House 183,
ALF HQ. Force B would cover their advance,
ile Force C set out to ambush all terrorist vehicles
the northern road. The attack force was
imately familiar with ALF HQ, having studied
ial photographs, and practised the assault on a
del of the ALF base for months. A wild fire-fight
ke out as the surprised terrorists were hit in a
htning assault. In all 13 terrorists were killed and
houses destroyed—and Misgav Am was
nged.

banon since 1982

en the IDF invaded Lebanon on 6 June 1982
nching Operation 'Peace for Galilee', SAYERET

**bloody conclusion of a SAYERET HARUV 'pursuit' of
estinian guerrillas in the Jordan Valley near the Allenby
dge, 18 June 1968. (IDF Spokesman)**

GOLANI was entrusted with the capture of the old
crusader fortress, Beaufort Castle. It had long been
used by the PLO as an artillery observation post, as
almost the entire Galilee region was visible from this
717m perch, symbolising the PLO dominance over
southern Lebanon. For SAYERET GOLANI, Beaufort
Castle had become an obsession. The unit studied
films of the position taken by Remote-Piloted
Vehicles (RPVs), closely examining the castle's
fortifications, trenches and communications system
and seeking out the best assault routes and
procedures.

On 6 June however, Chief of Staff 'Raful' Eitan
and OC Northern Command Maj.Gen. Drori
(GOLANI's OC in 1973) issued orders postponing the
assault on Beaufort: the IDF invasion routes
dictated bypassing the castle altogether. But the
orders were 'lost in channels'; and by 16:00 hours,
five hours behind schedule, the attack force reached
the pre-staging point. Led by Lt. Motti Goldman
and Capt. Gunni Harnik (who, awaiting his
discharge from the army, returned to the unit of his
own accord), the force consisted of men from
SAYERET GOLANI, who were to take the forward
positions, and HA'AN GOLANI, the brigade's sapper
force. The fighting was fierce, with the Palestinians
putting up a determined resistance; the GOLANI
soldiers had to 'purify' bunker after bunker with
grenades and automatic fire. Many of them ran out
of ammunition, and AK-47s were stripped from the
bodies of dead guerrillas. After six hours of brutal
combat, in which satchel charges were used to
breech the thick cement of the PLO positions, only
one machine gun bunker remained. Lt. Goldman
and Capt. Harnik advanced quickly, firing and
throwing over 30 grenades in the process. Harnik
was hit in the chest by an RPK burst; and in an act
of desperation, Lt. Goldman hurled a sapper's
charge towards the pit, destroying it in a cloud of
smoke and debris. A more symbolic than militarily
significant operation, the seizure of Beaufort Castle
cost the small, close-knit unit seven dead and 15
wounded.

Beaufort was only 'round one' for GOLANI in
Lebanon. GOLANI units were instrumental in
assisting paratroop and armoured forces to clear the
cities of Sidon and Damour, and in the eastern
sector a force from SAYERET GOLANI was heli-lifted to
the Beka'a Valley to join the fighting against the

Syrians. In an operation similar to the capture of Mt. Hermon and Beaufort Castle, SAYERET GOLANI led the brigade's successful capture of the Syrian intelligence-gathering position high atop Jebel Barouk from a determined Syrian commando force.

GOLANI was instrumental in the seizure of Kfar Sil, the Beirut suburb home of the PLO's command echelon. It was defended by a Syrian armoured and commando force, as well as 'commandos' from the PLO's crack 'Force 17'. Entering Kfar Sil, a mechanised GOLANI force was greeted by a murderous hail of anti-tank missile and small arms fire. The GOLANI units advanced, fighting their way into houses room by room, hand to hand. It took 19 hours for the battalion-size force to take control of Kfar Sil's kilometre-long main street; and Chief of Staff Eitan described the battle for Kfar Sil as the 'most brutal of the war'.

Kfar Sil gave easy access to Beirut International Airport; and GOLANI was once again assigned a difficult mission—to clear the slum neighbourhoods surrounding the airport of numerous PLO and leftist Muslim guerrilla defenders. The urban rubble provided perfect cover for the PLO anti-tank and sniper teams, who inflicted serious casualties on the GOLANI infantrymen. SAYERET GOLANI was called in, and with great care attacked each position as if it were assaulting a building

where hostages were being held. The neig bourhood was neutralised, and the airport seize

For three years following Operation 'Peace f Galilee', GOLANI units were highly active in the w against Shi'ite guerrillas in southern Lebano suffering dozens of casualties, and learning fi hand the 'art' of a brutal counter-insurgen campaign. GOLANI remains on Israel's northe border, and inside the 10km wide security zo inside Lebanon, fulfilling its obligation as guardia of Israel's northern frontier.

The Naval Commandos

The Naval Commandos trace their roots to t PAL'YAM of the pre-independence struggle. R cruited among PAL'MACH fighters from Palestin Mediterranean fishing villages, they receiv intensive underwater demolitions and amphibio assault training. The PAL'YAM assisted in bringing illegal Jewish immigrants, though its most famo operation was the doomed attempt by the '23 of t *Sea Lion*' to destroy the oil facilities at Tripoli 1941.

Following the Second World War, the PAL'Y

Defence Minister Moshe Dayan and KA'TZ'HA'R Brig.Gen. Eitan (right) address paratroops during large-scale exercises, 1968. He wears the olive 'Bar-Lev' jacket with 'jump school' unit tag sewn to the left sleeve and a red beret with General Staff badge. (IDF Archives)

A SAYERET TZANHANIM platoon commander apprehensiv examines a cave suspected of housing Palestinian guerril Jordan Valley, 5 November 1968. He wears olive fatigues, a web gear including a series of olive pouches for UZI magazin (IDF Archives)

nt into action against the British, its frogmen wing up several coastal launches and transports sting in deporting Jews to Cyprus. During the 8 War of Independence, the PAL'YAM became HEYL HAYAM, or IDF/Navy, with all nmando-type operations being conducted by the MMANDO YAMI (the Naval Commandos), and its all underwater demolitions unit. Considering ir limited manpower and resources, they ducted several spectacular operations, includ-the sinking of the Syrian supply ship *Lino Bari*, l the Egyptian Navy flagship *Emir Farouk* ploying Italian MTM-type explosive craft. lowing the war, the Naval Commandos rganised along the lines of the British SBS.

Volunteers for service in this prestigious unit lerwent a battery of brutal physical and chological tests before even being accepted for luation by KOMMANDO YAMI: acceptance did not arantee one's position with the unit, as 'weeding ' continued during 18 months of harsh training. is included everything from basic diving to high ed automobile driving skills. This recruitment cess, more stringent than that of any other IDF t apart from the pilots' course, assured the Naval mmandos of a proud and unique status.

Between 1953 and 1967 the KOMMANDO YAMI formed hundreds of operations against targets in ypt, Syria, Lebanon and points beyond. They re never officially mentioned in press despatches, l it was not until 1967 that the unit received icial notice'. On 5 June 1967, at 19:00 hours, six frogmen set out from the submarine INS *Tanin* to raid the port of Alexandria. The Egyptians expected an attack, and vigilant patrols in the surrounding waters, complete with depth charges, led to the capture of the six Israelis.

During the War of Attrition the KOMMANDO YAMI operated against conventional military and guerrilla targets; their two most famous operations were against the Egyptian facilities at Ras el-Adabi'a and Green Island in the summer of 1969. The objective of the 21 June raid on Ras el-Adabi'a was the destruction of the Egyptian air defence and coastal radar stations, guarded by over 30 Egyptian commandos. The attack force, led by Lt.Col. Zeev Almog, reached Ras el-Adabi'a by rubber dinghy, and after a 100m swim through the shallows, proceeded to attack the rader stations with complete success: 32 Egyptians were killed, 12 were wounded, and the radars were destroyed.

The success of the Ras el-Adabi'a raid enforced the preference of the General Staff for using the Naval Commandos rather than recon paratroop and infantry forces. Research following the operation indicated that the raiding party fired only three shots per Egyptian soldier killed, while in similar operations paratroopers unloaded two full magazines of ammunition for each enemy soldier killed. The KOMMANDO YAMI were able to reach their targets by swimming and diving, then

An intelligence photograph of Green Island, July 1969: note radar position at far right. (**IDF Archives**)

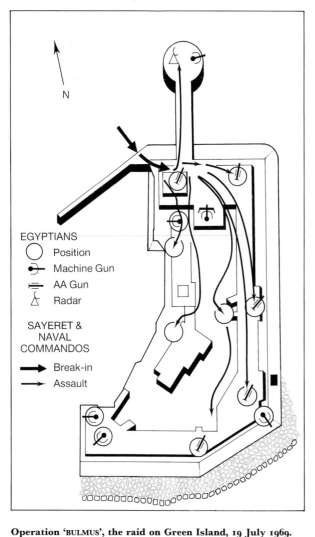

EGYPTIANS
○ Position
⊢ Machine Gun
⊨ AA Gun
△ Radar

SAYERET &
NAVAL
COMMANDOS

➡ Break-in
→ Assault

Operation 'BULMUS', the raid on Green Island, 19 July 1969.

attacking the target as a ground force; and it was argued that it was easier to train the Naval Commandos for land operations than to train the paratroopers to swim and dive.

In July 1969 the General Staff decided to strike at Green Island, a man-made island situated in the southern approach to the Suez Canal, 3km south of Port Ibrahim. It was 145m long by 65m wide, complete with an air defence radar and a fort, five AA gun emplacements containing 37mm and 85mm guns, and 14 guns of 14.5mm to 25mm calibre for local defence. A hundred soldiers defended Green Island, including an 'As-Sa'iqa' commando detachment. It was considered impregnable.

The raid was to be carried out by the Naval Commandos and SAYERET MAT'KAL (the paratroop

reconnaissance force of the General Staff). T Naval Commandos were to establish a beachhe at the northern point of the island, and attack garrison, while the SAYERET, landing from rub dinghies, were to act as cover and provide sappers.

At 23:00 hours on the night of 19–20 July Naval Commandos leapt out of the Zodiac cr and began their long swim towards Green Isla reaching the northern concrete slip below the rac tower two hours later. In complete silence, the s man assault team cut through the barbed w surrounding the tower at water level, undetec until an Egyptian sentry strolled by them, out fc quick smoke. He was quickly eliminated in a hai tracer fire which shattered the night's calm. Joir now by other Naval Commandos, the te operated with clockwork precision, storming a neutralising the enemy firing positions.

Egyptian fire was at first wild and not direct, I as a pitched battle developed heavy casualties w inflicted on the Naval Commandos. The hand-hand fighting on the fort's roof was the most vicic By now the SAYERET had reached the island, a joined the Naval Commandos in their attempts neutralise all enemy opposition. Lt.Col. Aln declared the island secured, and ordered SAYERET sappers to set the explosive charges. 02:55 hours, as the force set out back to base, t were followed by Egyptian shore guns, but also the sound of their explosives destroying much of island. Following the operation, KA'TZ'HA'R Ei called the Naval Commandos 'the élite young n of the State of Israel'.

The success of Operation 'BULMUS' ('Obsessio secured further employment for the Naval Cc mandos and on 7 September, the Egyptian na base at Ras Sadat was attacked and two P-torpedo boats sunk. Egyptian naval comman were also quite active during the War of Attriti sinking IDF/Navy vessels in the port of Ei Several KOMMANDO YAMI underwater demoliti experts were killed attempting to remove Egypt explosive devices from the hulls of ships. The f known action of the Naval Commandos was establishment of a beachhead for the re paratroop force in Operation 'BARDAS 54-55' 20–21 February 1973.

1: FO'SH fighter; Lower Galilee, 1937
2: PAL'MACHNIK, HAREL Bde.; Jerusalem, 1948
3: PAL'MACHNIKIT, NEGEV Bde., 1948

VOLSTAD

A

1: Paratrooper, 1950
2: Sergeant, paratroopers, 1951
3: Captain, 890th Para Bn., 1954

B

1: Commando, Unit 30, 1952
2: Commando, Unit 101, 1953
3: Paratrooper , 890th Para Bn., 1955

C

1: Paratrooper, 88th NA'HA'L Bn., 1956
2: Recon infantryman, SAYERET GOLANI, 1961
3: Recon paratrooper, SAYERET TZANHANIM, 1964

D

1: Paratrooper, 202nd Para Bn., 1966
2: Radioman, 55th Reserve Para Bde., 1967
3: Recon infantryman, SAYERET GOLANI, 1967

E

1: Paratrooper, HA'AN TZANHANIM, 1968
2: Captain, SAYERET HARUV, 1968
3: NA'HA'L paratrooper, 1969

F

1: Naval Commando, 1969
2: Recon paratrooper, SAYERET TZANHANIM, 1970
3: 2nd Lt., SAYERET EGOZ, 1972
4: Recon paratrooper, SAYERET MAT'KAL, 1972

G

1: 1st Lt., SAYERET SHIRION, 1970
2: Sgt. Candidate, SAYERET GOLANI, 1969
3: Naval Commando, 1972

H

1: Commando, SAYERET MAT'KAL, 1973
2: 2nd Lt., SAYERET GOLANI, 1973
3: Recon paratrooper, SAYERET SHAKED, 1973

I

J

1: 2nd Lt., YA'MA'M Border Guards, 1985
2: Cpl., 50th NA'HA'L Para Bn., 1986
3: Senior Master Sgt., SAYERET HADRUZIM, 1986

K

1: Parachute instructor, 1987
2: 1st Lt., IDF/AF Aeromed. Evac. Unit, 1987
3: Sgt., SHU'ALEI SHIMSHON 1987

L

During the 1973 War the Naval Commandos' que talents were once again needed. On the ht of 16–17 October four KOMMANDO YAMI nolitions experts made their way through the derwater net protecting Port Said: one pair ached mines to two Egyptian landing craft, but other pair, tragically, never returned from the ration.

he Egyptian naval base at A'ardaqa was no nger to the KOMMANDO YAMI. On 9, 11, and 18 tober 1973 Naval Commandos attacked the e, succeeding in sinking a 'Komar' Fast Attack aft. On the night of 21 October, OC IDF/Navy j.Gen. Binyamin Telem ordered that LAW i-tank rockets be rushed to the Naval Com- ndos in Sinai: A'ardaqa was to be hit yet again. 22:00 hours on 21 October a Naval Commando ce set out on their mission, the destruction of ther 'Komar' at A'ardaqa. After a six-hour rney, the commandos managed to get within m of the advancing ship. They were spotted, wever, and the shore batteries opened up on the nmandos, who now closed the range to 40m. All LAWs fired missed their marks, except for the one they had, which scored a direct hit, turning 'Komar' into a ball of flame. Intelligence orts later confirmed a symbolic finale to the ration. The 'Komar' that had been sunk was the which, six years earlier on 21 October 1967, d the salvo of 'Styx' missiles which sank the F/Navy flagship INS *Eilat*; and exactly 25 years lier, the commander of the raid on A'ardaqa, j.Gen.(Res.) Yochai Ben-Nun, had com- nded the operation which resulted in the sinking the *Emir Farouk*.

n the IDF's campaign against terrorism, the MMANDO YAMI has made numerous raids against estinian targets in Lebanon and throughout the ddle East. On the night of 8 June 1978 a team ded the PLO Naval Commando base at Dahr el- rj in Lebanon, destroying numerous buildings d killing dozens of terrorists. In fact, the Naval mmandos enjoyed making routine landings ng the Lebanon coast, a habit which came in ful on the night of 6–7 June 1982, when OC F/Navy Maj.Gen. Zeev Almog ordered the MMANDO YAMI to prepare a bridgehead on the -Awali coast for the largest amphibious landing IDF history.

Most of the KOMMANDO YAMI's operations since have remained highly classified, the aura of secrecy surrounding the unit contributing to their mystique as well as to their operational survival.

Territorial and other Reconnaissance Units

In addition to 'regular' paratroop and infantry reconnaissance units, the IDF maintains several territorial and other recon commando formations.

SAYERET SHAKED

The oldest of the three territorial paratroop reconnaissance forces, SAYERET SHAKED ('Almond') was Southern Command's response to Arab guerrilla and Egyptian Military Intelligence in-

Recon paratroopers from SAYERET EGOZ prepare for a night ambush inside Lebanese territory, January 1969. The FN rifleman still wears his black beret with infantry beret badge on red background; and tan-khaki web gear over his olive field jacket. The soldier at right wears the 'Bar-Lev' jacket and woollen balaclava/cap, and carries the magazines for his AK-47 in a captured khaki canvas pouch. (IDF Archives)

Wearing tan-khaki field jackets, NA'HA'L paratroopers prepare for their journey home following the successful completion of Operation 'TARNEGOL 53', 27 December 1969—the capture of the P-12 radar at Ras Arab. (IDF Archives)

filtration in the Negev Desert. The successors to the GIVA'ATI Bde.'s recon force SHU'ALEI SHIMSHON, SHAKED patrolled the desert on foot, by jeep and even on camel. It was a truly integrated unit, and its most famous commander was Lt.Col. Amos Yarkoni, a Bedouin, who prior to 1948 had even taken part in anti-Jewish guerrilla activities. The Bedouins brought to SHAKED the inherited arts of desert tracking and warfare.

During the 1967 War the unit was split into small sections, acting as reconnaissance scouts to the IDF divisions advancing into Sinai. The first recon force to engage Egyptian commandos on the east bank of the Canal during the War of Attrition, it initiated hundreds of 'pursuits' along the Canal, and in the Arava Desert near Jordan. These anti-terrorist/commando operations transformed the small unit into an élite strike force, mobilised at a moment's notice for the most difficult of tasks. During the anti-terrorist campaign in Gaza, 1970–73, SHAKED performed brilliantly, utilising its speed and integrated manpower with astounding results.

SHAKED participated in the early containment battles against the Egyptians in the 1973 War, eventually crossing the Canal to battle Egyptian commandos. It last saw combat during the 1982 Lebanon War as a mechanised recon force, participating in, among other actions, the blood-letting at the Ein el-Hilweh refugee camp. It was disbanded in 1983, its command echelon forming the nucleus of the reborn GIVA'ATI Infantry Brigade.

SAYERET EGOZ

In 1956 OC Northern Command Gen. Yitzh[a]k Rabin ordered the formation of SAYERET EGO[Z] ('Walnut'), a Command reconnaissance force [to] secure the northern frontier and act as t[he] Command's mobile intelligence-gathering unit[: a] monumental task for a unit numbering only [—] soldiers and three Bedouin trackers. In 1965, M[aj.] Haim Sela was appointed EGOZ's commander; [an] ex-NA'HA'L and GOLANI officer, Sela transform[ed] EGOZ into a 'fighting battalion', and during t[he] 1967 War led in the capture of Kuneitra[1].

Following the 1967 War, EGOZ faced its m[ost] challenging operational task, preventing terror[ist] infiltration from northern Jordan, Syria a[nd] Lebanon. This stretched EGOZ's manpower to t[he] limit, and it was the norm for an EGOZ fighter [to] participate in over 300 ambushes a year! EGOZ w[as] involved in countless cross-river operations, hitti[ng] training and staging areas across the Yarmou[k,] Jordan, and Litani rivers. Its most famo[us] operational zone was Lebanon, and EGOZ fighte[rs] endured harsh climatic conditions in their hundre[ds] of spectacular raids against terrorist bases. Th[eir] largest raid was Operation 'KALAHAT 4' in t[he] autumn of 1972, a direct response to the murder [of] 11 Israeli athletes at Munich; this involved t[he] entire SAYERET, as well as elements from GOLANI a[nd] the BARAK Armoured Brigade. SAYERET EGOZ w[as] disbanded in 1973.

SAYERET HARUV

In 1966 Chief of Staff Lt.Gen. Yitzhak Rab[in] authorised the formation of a Central Comma[nd] reconnaissance force known as SAYERET HARU[V] ('Carob'), to operate along the Jordanian bord[er.] During the 1967 War a HARUV task force attempt[ed] to seize el-Fatah commander 'Abu Ammar' (Ya[sser] Arafat), who fled Ramallah for safe haven [in] Jordan. Following the war HARUV became HATIV[AT] HABIKA'A's élite strike force, taking the forefront [in] the desert pursuits of guerrilla infiltrators. The u[nit] received little rest or reward for their daily a[nd] costly operations, though many new voluntee[rs] chose HARUV for the challenge it posed. By 1968 t[he] security situation in the Jordan Valley warrant[ed] the unit's expansion, and HARUV became

---

[1]In 1982 Col.(Res.) Sela was killed in action just south of Beirut.

talion, incorporating into its arsenal new
apons systems including Bell-205 helicopters,
infra-red and electronic detection devices.
HARUV's pursuits in the Jordan Valley took a
sh toll on the small unit, which suffered heavy
ualties, especially among its officers. One such
ualty was HARUV commander, Lt.Col. Tzvi Ofer
YERET GOLANI commander during the Nuqieb
1), killed during a pursuit in Wadi Kelet on 20
cember 1968: like Lt.Col. Regev and Lt. Manela
ore him, Ofer paid the price so often demanded
an élite unit commander in the IDF. HARUV's
st impressive tally was achieved just prior to
ependence Day 1969 when, in a series of well-
cuted ambushes, it terminated 23 infiltration
empts, killing 21 guerrillas in the process. HARUV
ssed the border into Jordan on countless
asions, many times in week-long operations deep
enemy territory. During the 1973 War HARUV
ght with Maj.Gen. Adan Bren's division near
ez. In the last two days of fighting HARUV—a unit

which never exceeded 1,000 men—lost 33 dead.
Following the war HARUV was sent in against
terrorists in Gaza, ending an era for the unit. Its
mission in the Jordan Valley had been accomplished, with the most desirable reward of all: peace
on the frontier.

SAYERET HADRUZIM

Druze, Bedouin and Circassian Muslims have
volunteered into the IDF ever since the in-
corporation of the *Arab el-Hai'b* Bedouin tribe into
the PAL'MACH (forming the PAL'*Hai'b*) during the
1948 War. They were basically segregated into
'Minorities Unit 300', though outstanding soldiers
were accepted into the territorial reconnaissance
formations, as well as into the ranks of the GOLANI
Brigade. The Druze distinguished themselves as far
more than token trackers and Arab soldiers of

An excellent study of a SAYERET GOLANI radioman firing his UZI
in 'Fatahland', January 1970. Note AN/PRC-25 carried on an
infantry packboard inside a tan rucksack. (IDF Archives)

Recon paratroopers from SAYERET TZANHANIM wearing specially designed olive nylon 'commando' web gear (the forerunner of the IDF load-bearing equipment worn today) prepare to be heli-lifted home following Operation 'RODOS', the day-long raid against the Egyptian garrison at Shedwan Island, 22 January 1970. Note Super Frelon helicopter with IAF markings. (IGPO)

fortune; and in 1959 they were paid the compliment of being conscripted into military service.

Many Druze advanced quickly in the IDF and National Police Border Guards, achieving senior ranks. The notion for a separate Druze reconnaissance unit was the brainchild of Maj.(Res.) Muhamad Mulah, a fiercely loyal officer, who was determined not to waste his people's combat potential. Following the 1967 War, Maj. Mulah presented a plan to Chief of Staff Lt.Gen. Haim Bar-Lev calling for the formation of a Druze paratroop recon unit, able to parachute into the Druze areas in Syria should war with Syria break out. Bar-Lev liked the idea, and SAYERET HADRUZIM was born.

SAYERET HADRUZIM's operational zone was the northern frontier. It served as a symbol of pride to young Druze conscripts, who considered [t]wearing of the SAYERET HADRUZIM reconnaissa[nce] wings a more prized status than being a 'regu[lar] IDF unit tracker. During the 1982 Lebanon W[ar] SAYERET HADRUZIM served with distinction, prov[ing] its élite status during the difficult campaign agai[nst] Palestinian guerrillas. Lebanon was a difficult [place] for the Druze: Lebanon's Druze community w[as] often at odds with occupying IDF, and the Shi['ite] Muslims viewed the Druze as 'infidels' or n[on-]believers, and often targeted SAYERET HADRUZ[IM] personnel and patrols for the harshest of terro[rist] attacks. Nevertheless, not one Druze refused serv[ice] in Lebanon throughout the three year I[DF] presence.

SAYERET MAT'KAL

SAYERET MAT'KAL is certainly the most mysteriou[s of] all the IDF's élite units; its organisation, train[ing] routine, and operational history remain hig[hly] classified, and official mentions are rare. Commo[nly] referred to as the 'Chief of Staff's Boys', SAYER[ET] MAT'KAL (General Staff Reconnaissance) is

...DF's covert response to the most dire national ...curity needs. Their *rumoured* exploits know no ...ounds, ranging from leading the IDF raid at ...ntebbe, to assisting MOSSAD hit teams in Europe. ...heir first official recognition followed the assault ... Green Island.

On 8 May 1972, four 'Black September' terrorists ...ncluding two women) hijacked a Belgian Sabena ...eing 707 on a routine flight from Brussels to Lod. ...udaciously landing in Israel, the terrorists ...manded the release of 100 imprisoned Arabs in ...change for not blowing up the aircraft. The IDF ...sponse was immediate, and General Staff ...perations chief Col. Emmanuel Shaked sum-...oned the 'Chief of Staff's Boys' led by Maj. Ehud ...arak. The men of SAYERET MAT'KAL had trained ...r months for the possibility of dealing with a ...jacked airliner; and while Defence Minister ...ayan played for time, entering into false ...gotiations with the terrorists, the commandos ...actised their assault techniques on an EL AL 707 at ...e Israel Aircraft Industries terminal nearby.

The first stage of the operation was the immobilisation of the aircraft by a commando team complemented by EL AL technicians, who drained the hydraulic fluid from the undercarriage and the brakes. Next, a busload of 'Arab prisoners' (actually dark-complexioned Israeli soldiers with shaven heads) was brought to within eyesight of the cockpit to give the terrorists the feeling of imminent victory. Meanwhile, in the airport's main terminal, the commando team received its final briefing for the rescue mission. They were to burst through the three emergency exit doors in groups of four, eliminate the terrorists immediately, and evacuate the aircraft. All the commandos wore white EL AL technicians' overalls, and carried 9mm Berettas.

The terrorists, confident of their victory, granted permission for the aircraft to be serviced for flight. As the Defence Minister, Chief of Staff, and dozens of senior officers observed from the watchtower, the

49

commandos headed towards the Boeing on EL AL tractors. At 16:10 hours on 9 May the explosive charges applied to the exits detonated, and the commandos entered the aircraft. Amongst the confusion and smoke, they proceeded to kill the two male terrorists and wounded the two women, in just 34 seconds! The next day the press made no mention of the unit, identifying them only as the 'angels in white'.

The following month the 'angels in white' struck against terrorism again, though this time in a more unconventional manner. Operation 'ARGAZ BET' on 26 June 1972 was a classic commando operation intended to expose the Syrian connection with terrorist acts against Israel. The objective: to kidnap five ranking Syrian Military Intelligence officers in southern Lebanon and hold them as

'human ransom' for three IAF pilots held in Syri and Egyptian jails. The raiding party was hai picked, and read like a 'Who's Who' of the ID élite, including Maj. Ehud Barak (a former head Military Intelligence, the current deputy Chief Staff, and the IDF's most decorated soldier), Cap Yoni Netanyahu and Muki Batzar (later grou force and deputy commanders at Entebbe). N since the times of Meir Har-Zion had a comman force been used to kidnap enemy soldie Operation 'ARGAZ BET' was carried out by (commandos supported by armoured, SAYER GOLANI and EGOZ elements. After a brief fire-fig five Syrian officers, including a major-general, we POWs: weeks later the pilots were released.

On 10 April 1973 the commandos once again I a large-scale IDF assault, this time in Operati 'AVIV NE'URIM'. On 10 April at 01:30 hours, a tes of 30 MOSSAD agents, SAYERET commandos, a recon paratroopers slipped ashore on Beirut's Dc Beach secured by Naval Commandos, and we driven to their targets in cars rented by fell MOSSAD agents[1]. 'Force ALEPH', commanded Maj. Barak, proceeded towards the apartme complex housing three of 'Black September's' t ranking officials, killed them, and relieved t premises of its memos and files. 'Force B (including a HA'AN TZANHANIM contingent) atta ked the headquarters of the DFLP, while a th group attacked 'Black September's' Beirut bor factory. IAF fighters flew cover overhead, wh helicopters evacuated the dead and wound helped remove captured files, and dropped spik 'crows' feet' to prevent Palestinian road pursuit the attack force. It was Israel's most spectacul response to terrorism, and the last which has ev been officially attributed to SAYERET MAT'KAL.

* * *

The IAF's Aeromedical Evacuation U (AEU), and the National Police Border Guard YA'MA'M (anti-terrorist unit) have emerged as sma embryonic élite forces whose performance in t Lebanon war was highly impressive. Although function is to rescue downed pilots in enem territory, the AEU succeeded in evacuating 2,5 IDF casualties from battlefields throughout Le

Commandos from SAYERET MAT'KAL evacuate the passengers of the *Sabena* Boeing 707 at Lod Airport, following the successful storming of the airliner on 9 May 1972. Note 'white angel' on steps, still clutching his Beretta M1951S. (IGPO)

[1]Maj. Barak awaited the commandos in a rented car disguised a blonde woman!

on, bringing them to hospitals in Israel in record ...e. The unit is a highly professional and secretive ...ce, made up almost exclusively of NCOs and ...icers. Only the best helicopter pilots are allowed ... volunteer for the unit, in which all must undergo ... gruelling 'modified' paratroop basic training, ...lowed by intense medical, survival, and combat ...ining. Most recently, in a dramatic rescue ...eration, the AEU recovered a downed F-4 pilot ... southern Lebanon on 16 October 1986 in a ...sperate race against time, with the pilot clinging ... dear life to a Bell-209 Cobra all the way back to ...ael.

The YA'MA'M was formed after the Munich ...ympics massacre, and has developed into one of ...e world's best police anti-terrorist formations, ...ining, among others, West Germany's GSG-9. ...t part of the IDF proper, the YA'MA'M joined ...er Border Guard units in Lebanon when IDF ...mmanders found themselves incapable of dealing ...th the Palestinian and Muslim guerrilla threat. ...e YA'MA'M led the Border Guard effort in this ...en brutal war of pursuits and ambushes; and ...hough they numbered less than one per cent of ...e total Israeli invasion force, they captured over ... per cent of all the top Palestinian terrorist ...mmanders in southern Lebanon.

In 1987, however, it appears that a relatively ...ung unit has wrested a place among the IDF's ...te. The GIVA'ATI Infantry Brigade was re-...ivated in late 1983 as a marine-type strike force, ...lowing the successful amphibious landings on the ...ast of Sidon in 1982. The brigade and its ...connaissance battalion SHU'ALEI SHIMSHON, like ...LANI before it, trained twice as hard as other units ... prove itself—a feat accomplished successfully, ...ce in the years which followed it beat both the ...ratroops and GOLANI in brigade-level exercises, as ...ll as performing brilliantly at the difficult security ...ks in southern Lebanon. GIVA'ATI was rewarded ... its efforts and new-found élite status, receiving its ...n distinctive purple beret.

The Plates

With cloth covering his face from dust as well as providing a certain degree of anonymity, a SAYERET GOLANI platoon commander co-ordinates his unit's movement during a raid against Palestinian guerrilla targets in southern Lebanon, July 1972. He wears olive fatigues including three-pocket trousers, and Israeli M-1 helmet fitted with tan netting secured by rubber tubing. The rank of SEGEN is indicated by the khaki shoulder strap slides with two green stencilled bars. Note captured AK ammo pouch worn across shoulder, and German military flashlight. (IDF Archives)

kolpak hat had been adopted by the NOTRIM, or Jewish Settlement Police, and since many FO'SH fighters were NOTRIM themselves, it was worn on many patrols, as were British sun helmets or bush hats. The ammunition pouches are also of British origin, though HAGANAH workshops copied them in cheaper forms. The .303 SMLE and khaki drill shorts were probably stolen from a drunken Tommy in Tel Aviv by one of the many HAGANAH 'acquisition units'. The FO'SH were the best-equipped of HAGANAH units at the time, presenting an identifiable military appearance. Of interest is the Lewis gun—rare and risked only when heavily-armed Arab opposition was expected.

A2: PAL'MACHNIK, HAREL Brigade, Jerusalem, 1948
The departure of the British 6th Airborne Division from Palestine in 1948 coincided with the

: FO'SH fighter, Lower Galilee, 1937
...te combination of civilian, British, and ...GANAH-produced articles. The Turkish style

acquisition by the PAL'MACH of the majority of its military clothing. The Denison smock, woollen 'cap comforter', and camouflage 'face veil' are worn with US Army ammunition pouches and civilian khaki trousers. This fighter carries a Lee Enfield Mk.IV rifle fitted with a sniper-scope and a flame-thrower produced by the IRGUN TZAVA LEUMI, the right-wing terror group led by Menachem Begin. Though the PAL'MACH and the IRGUN were at the opposite ends of the political spectrum, wartime needs sometimes necessitated sharing equipment. Note the German P-38 pistol and Mills grenade worn on the belt.

Paratroopers from SAYERET TZANHANIM prepare to move out against Egyptian positions at the Chinese Farm, 16 October 1973. Note grenadier carrying rifle grenades in his tan canvas '37 small pack, and propellant cartridges attached to his web gear. The soldier with the RPG-7 carries the rockets in a captured ammunition bag, later reproduced by the IDF Ordnance Corps when the IDF absorbed the weapon into full line service. (IDF Archives)

A3: PAL'MACHNIKIT, NEGEV Brigade; Negev Desert, 19
This PAL'MACHNIKIT wears a typical assortment left over British and indigenous articles. The e British battledress blouse was probably retriev from the trash bin of a military base, while the ' webbing equipment was purchased on Palestin thriving 'black market'. Ammunition for t HAGANAH copy of the Sten Mk.II 9mm su machine gun is carried in a tan canvas Germ MP40 pouch. Equipment from all over the wor was seen in the 1948 War of Independence, HAGANAH agents abroad sent home any type military equipment they could find, ranging fro canteen covers to fighter planes. The .303 SMI has been fitted with a HAGANAH device for firi Mills grenades: the HAGANAH loved to 'tinker', a their infant arms industry managed to produ everything from nail bombs to mortars made fro sewage pipes.

: Paratrooper, 1950

he most pressing problem the first paratroopers
ced was the acquisition of safe parachutes: unable
afford new equipment, they were forced to jump
th second-hand 'chutes which had been on their
ay to the shirt factory! Needless to say, training
talities were demoralisingly high. This TZANHAN's
rachuting gear is entirely British: a British jump
lmet (with crudely stencilled IDF parachutist
ngs), and a British X-type parachute. The tan-
aki fatigues (an ironed and pressed version of
hich doubled for the soldier's Class A uniform) are
raeli-produced, and worn with an olive fatigue
eater. The weapon is an MP40.

: Paratrooper, 1951

he of the earliest Class A uniforms adopted by the
ratroopers was the sand khaki shirt and
users, adorned with cloth parachutist wings
placed in 1953 by the metal variant worn to this
y). The red beret, infantry HEYL RAGLIM beret
dge (with red plastic backing indicating combat
vice), and brown leather paratroop boots are all
sic elements of the paratrooper's uniform worn to
s day. This sergeant or SAMAL (note crude
rizontal stripes) also wears the 1948 campaign
bon above the left breast pocket. The Czecho-
vak K98 7.92mm Mauser rifle, fitted with an
aeli-produced bayonet, was the most common
apon of the period.

: Captain, 890th Paratroop Battalion, 1954

e Battledress Class A uniform was standard issue
the IDF until the mid-1970s (the Air Force was
ued with a blue-grey version, the Navy with a
vy blue equivalent). It was a direct copy of the
itish uniform, though the climate faded it to an
ve appearance. The embroidered 'snake and
ngs' unit patch sewn to the upper left arm at first
resented the 890th Para Bn., and has been
ained by the progressively re-numbered 'regular
ny' paratroop brigade to this day. The dark olive
and white shirt were restricted to special
casions, and were seldom seen after 1954. The
tal parachutist wings are worn with a blue
ckground; and the red lanyard represents
tructor status. The rank of SEREN is indicated by
ee bronze metal bars with a pressed sword and
f crest, worn on a red background on dark olive

A SAYERET GOLANI squad engages Syrian commandos near the
IDF observation post atop Mt. Hermon, 21 October 1973. The
foreground man has inserted padding under his heavy
ammunition pouches. (IDF Archives)

shoulder strap slides. The IDF brass pins are worn
on both collar points with red backing, and were
required on all Battledress Class A uniforms.

C1: Commando, Unit 30; Hebron, 1952

The Unit 30 commandos were regarded as
partisans and guerrillas, and they behaved in such a
manner. Military discipline was non-existent, as
was military dress on or off base. In the field they
wore whatever suited their needs best, from
Bedouin garb to camouflage uniforms bought
commercially. This commando, face blackened for
a night ambush, wears a British-style knitted 'cap
comforter', a British 1942 windproof camouflage
smock, and tan Israeli fatigue trousers with two
large cargo pockets. An Israeli copy of the British
'37 large pack carries the .303 Bren gun
ammunition.

C2: Commando, Unit 101; Samua, 1953

Like the men of Unit 30, Unit 101 seldom wore
proper military attire on or off base. This led to
several nasty confrontations with the Military
Police, making the latter as unpopular with Unit
101 as the Jordanian Arab Legion! This commando
on an ambush against Jordanian positions near
Samua wears a typical assortment of uniform items.

The SAYERET GOLANI task force which rescued the nursery at Kibbutz Misgav Am reconstruct their assault for the benefit of the press. Note Kevlar bulletproof assault vests with built-in canteen and communications gear pouches. The assault leader carries a Beretta M1951S and the soldiers UZIS, as the close-quarter battle did not justify the use of the GALIL assault rifle. (IMoD)

The battledress jacket is worn here complete with parachutist wings. The plain white *kefiyeh* doubled as a scarf, and a simple disguise. The .45 Thompson gun, here with two magazines taped together, was a favoured weapon, as was the German MP40 9mm sub-machine gun. Indigenous Israeli web gear is worn, most notably the tan-khaki canvas pouch for holding the Tommy-gun magazines, which was later developed to carry magazines for the UZI—yet to enter full service. A K98 bayonet is tucked into the pistol belt. The bush hat was the preferred headgear of '101', in direct reference to the SNS and PAL'MACH.

C3: Paratrooper, 890th Paratroop Battalion; Kilkil 1955

This paratrooper carries an interesting product IDF Ordnance Corps 'tinkering', a K98 fitted wi a grenade-firing device, seen here with an Isra Military Industries anti-tank rifle grenade. T khaki fatigue uniform is standard for the peric worn here with British '37 web gear including t large pack, and US-style Israeli-produced cantee The US M-1 helmet has been crudely fitted wi tan camouflage netting, and tan leggings are wc with the brown leather paratroop boots.

D1: Paratrooper, 88th NA'HA'L Battalion; Mitla Pass, October 1956

This illustrates the marked improvement weaponry and equipment issued to the Isra soldier since the inception of the IDF in 1948. I uniform consists of Israeli olive fatigue trousers w two large cargo pockets, and Israeli-produced fi jacket and brown paratroop boots. The Brit jump helmet has been fitted with tan netting h by tan rubber tubing. His web gear consists o pouch for carrying up to 10 magazines for his 9n UZI sub-machine gun, and a grenade pouch. Smith & Wesson No.2 .380 revolver is carried in khaki canvas holster, and a commercial knife mi also be worn on the pistol belt. The UZI, seen h fitted with the early wooden stock, was ma famous by the paratroopers at Mitla.

D2: Recon infantryman, SAYERET GOLANI; Nuqieb, 1

The GOLANI Bde's raid on the fortified Syr positions at Nuqieb marked GOLANI's acceptanc an élite unit—especially its reconnaissance b talion, SAYERET GOLANI. This recon infantrym wears the standard olive fatigue blouse and trous black combat boots, and fatigue sweater. T Israeli-produced pouches were specifically desig to carry the Israeli produced 7.62mm FN F. assault rifle magazines. A '37 small pack ho explosives; note also that two canteens were wo Many GOLANI soldiers placed grenades inside th canteen pouches after the heavy mud encounte at Nuqieb made drinking from those cante unsafe.

D3: Recon paratrooper, SAYERET TZANHANIM, 1964

During 1956–1967 France was Israel's larg

A SAYERET TZANHANIM squad prepares to storm a PFLP-GC stronghold near Sidon, 7 June 1982. They wear the new EPHOD or web gear, Kevlar flak vests, and crudely camouflaged Kevlar infantry ballistic helmets, and carry GALIL (long barrelled with bipod) and GLILON (short-barrelled) 5.56mm assault rifles. Note squad medic carrying stretcher on an infantry packboard, and squad gunner with FN MAG 7.62mm light machine gun with khaki canvas ammunition bag. (IMoD)

pplier of military equipment; and one of the most ught-after items was the 'lizard-pattern' mouflage fatigue uniform, issued only to élite its. The IDF had always been apprehensive out camouflage, but the free offer of large stocks uniforms (of both French airborne and general rvice types) was too tempting for the budget-nscious IDF to ignore. They remained in active rvice until 1968, when Palestinian guerrillas gan wearing the same or very similar uniforms. his SEGEN (first lieutenant) wears the lizard-ttern fatigue blouse and trousers. Rank is dicated by the 'out of uniform' Class A bronze etal bars with red background on tan field slides. he EFA-672-12 (IS) main parachute with 'line st canopy deployment' is worn, as is the T-10-R S) reserve. An Israeli-produced 3.5 in. bazooka is rried in the tan canvas weapon bag, and a smaller nmunition bag is worn under the reserve 'chute; te the folding-stock UZI. Note the M-1 helmet ted with tan netting, supporting the soldier's aily fix' of cigarettes.

E1: Paratrooper, 202nd Paratroop Battalion; Samua, 13 November 1966
This corporal returning from Operation 'MAGRESA' wears an interesting combination of a lizard-pattern smock over an IDF so-called 'battledress jacket' with black fur collar. Underneath is the olive issue fatigue uniform; web gear consists of the UZI ammunition pouch, grenade pouch, and holster for a Beretta M1951 9mm pistol.

E2: Radioman, 55th Reserve Paratroop Brigade; Jerusalem, June 1967
Advancing through the Old City of Jerusalem, he wears a US M1943 field jacket over French lizard-pattern fatigues. An AN/PRC-10 radio is carried on an infantry packboard, with the handset hooked to

Two soldiers from SAYERET GOLANI watch a suspect building on the outskirts of Kfar Sil, 12 June 1982. The NCO (*right*) wears OG-106 Nomex trousers and Kevlar flak vest, while the officer (*left*) wears olive fatigues, flak vest, and EPHOD gear. Note Orlite infantry ballistic helmet. (IDF Spokesman)

the straps of the tan-netted British jump helmet. A wide array of pouches were carried, including standard IDF canteens, FN, grenade, and US M1943 bandage pouch. The UZI often had two magazines clipped together, crucial for quick reloading during fire-fights.

E3: Recon infantryman, SAYERET GOLANI; Tel Fahar, 8 June 1967

This soldier from the 'Flying Leopards' wears the lizard-pattern camouflage fatigue uniform with the Israeli 'battledress' jacket, worn here as a vest with sleeves crudely removed. The practice of altering uniforms was limited to élite units, who were less likely to be punished upon returning damaged uniforms at the end of their three year service. The weapon is the heavy-barrel squad support FN FAL with bipod; cloth has been wrapped around the barrel and butt to minimize impact noise during movement. The web gear consists of four khaki canvas FN ammunition pouches, and a holster for a Beretta M1951S 9mm pistol.

F1: Paratrooper, HA'AN TZANHANIM; Beirut International Airport, 28 December 1968

As no civilians were meant to be hurt in the raid which resulted in the destruction of 13 MEA airliners, paratroop brigade commander Col. Rafael Eitan decided that his men would appear less threatening if dressed in their 'Class A's'—red berets and all! This paratrooper from HA'AN

TZANHANIM (the paratroop brigade's demoliti[c] unit) wears the olive four-pocket paratroop Clas[s] smock, called the YARKIT. Basic parachutist wi[n] are worn with blue (regular) background, as is [the] 1967 campaign ribbon, both above the left bre[ast] pocket. The three-pocket Class A trousers [a] baggier and finer cotton-blend version of the thr[ee] pocket fatigue trousers) are issued only [to] paratroopers and GOLANI infantrymen. The R[us]sian AK-47 7.62mm assault rifle was captured [in] such great numbers from the Syrians, Egyptia[ns] and Palestinians that it became standard issue [for] IDF élite units.

F2: Captain, SAYERET HARUV; Jordan Valley, 1968

Although the guerrilla threat posed to the Jord[an] Valley following the 1967 conquest of the W[est] Bank prompted the IDF to establish the 'Jord[an] Valley Paratroop Brigade', it was SAYER[ET] HARUV—the reconnaissance paratroop battalion [of] the IDF Central Command—which led [the] campaign to halt guerrilla infiltration across [the] border. This captain, leading his squad to [the] demolition of a suspected guerrilla hide-out ca[ve] (always a tricky and costly operation), carries [a] portion of the unit's explosives in a green nylon sa[ck]. He carries the Chinese version of the AK-47, fit[ted] with a folding bayonet, as well as a PPSH-[41] liberated from a guerrilla along the way. The oli[ve] fatigue blouse has TZAHAL (Hebrew acronym [for] Israel Defense Forces) stencilled above the [left] breast pocket. The AK magazines are carried i[n]

A paratroop patrol moves through an unidentified Sh[ia] village in southern Lebanon in their heavily armed je[ep] February 1985. They wear the BEGED HOREF winter cover[alls] underneath rain smocks, infantry ballistic helmets, [and] goggles. (Asher Koralik-IDF Spokesman)

n canvas pouch captured from Palestinian errillas, though later produced in Israel. A US rmy flashlight is tucked into the web gear, as is a ap. The olive fatigue 'baseball' or 'B-Class' cap is orn; this was issued in great numbers following the 67 War.

: NA'HA'L paratrooper, Ras Arab; 29 October 1969

his paratrooper, involved in some of the versionary demolitions ops around the radar se's perimeter during Operation 'TARNEGOL 53' Chicken 53') wears an olive field jacket which has en bleached tan to resemble an Egyptian iform. He carries three loads of explosives secured an infantry packboard by rope. The load-aring equipment shown here developed years er into the web gear currently worn by the IDF. nsisting of lightweight nylon pouches, its ymmetrical arrangement affords maximum com- rt in any firing position. This system was iginated by recon paratroopers, who made crude t comfortable pouches out of cut-up fatigues. The N MAG 7.62mm light machine gun has been in DF service since the mid-1960s and remains one of e most popular and reliable weapons in the Israeli ventory. Note IDF-issue knee pads.

: Naval commando, Green Island; 20 July 1969

his KOMMANDO YAMI wears a specially designed ack neoprene rubber summer diving suit, as well as the dark green/grey neoprene rubber equipment vest which was specifically designed by the naval commandos for use on short-duration raids. It consists of waterproof pouches for up to ten UZI magazines, five grenades, and medical and signal equipment. The UZI 9mm SMG with folding stock is carried, and a commercial diver's knife is attached to the right leg.

G2: Recon paratrooper, SAYERET TZANHANIM; Shedwan Island, 22 January 1970

Most IDF combat soldiers possess a double, sometimes even triple weapons rôle. This squad grenadier (note anti-personnel and anti-tank rifle grenades carried) is also the squad medic (note medic's pouch worn on pistol belt). A '37 small pack holding a supply of rifle grenades is worn in addition to the 'commando' load-bearing equip-ment. Note blinker strobe light attached to the M-1 helmet, which is fitted with tan netting supported by black rubber tubing and has a diagonal strip of white tape for station-keeping.

G3: Second Lieutenant, SAYERET EGOZ; Southern Lebanon, 1972

During the years following the 1967 War, SAYERET EGOZ, the reconnaissance paratroop battalion of the IDF's Northern Command, initiated many week-long ambushes deep inside Lebanon's guerrilla territory. This SEGEN MISHNE wears a US M-65 field jacket over his olive fatigue blouse and US OG-107 fatigue trousers. Foam lining is placed beneath the web gear for comfort. A '37 small pack holds extra ammunition and rations. A US Marine K-Bar knife is crudely attached to the right leg with cloth, and a strobe light is attached to the netted M-1 helmet. Rank is indicated by light tan cloth shoulder strap slides with one green stencilled bar. Note AK-47 with folding stock.

G4: Recon paratrooper, SAYERET MATKAL; Lod Airport, 21 May 1972

This member of the IDF's most secretive commando force, preparing to storm the hijacked Sabena airliner, wears white mechanic's coveralls over his olive fatigues. The brown paratroop boots have been quickly polished black, giving a purple appearance, and the weapon used in the assault is the Beretta M1951S.

H1: First Lieutenant, SAYERET SHIRION, 1970

SAYERET SHIRION, the IDF Armoured Corps reconnaissance and mobile anti-tank battalion, was one of the IDF's crack units. They were transferred from division to division depending on where and

when their skills were needed. Their main weapo[n] was the jeep-mounted 106mm recoilless rif[le] though SAYERET SHIRION often used tanks in lon[g] range reconnaissance rôles. Eventually, they we[re] disbanded, and switched over to the control of t[he] paratroopers, where they serve today in SAYER[ET] OREV.

Although considered an élite unit, the men [of] SAYERET SHIRION wore average Armoured Cor[ps] Class A uniforms, including the unpopular Gene[ral] Services side-pocket trousers. SAYERET SHIRI[ON] recon wings (an advancing winged tank) are wo[rn] with the green backing indicating reconnaissan[ce] duty above the left breast pocket, and below t[he] basic parachutist wings. The black beret bears t[he] Armoured Corps beret badge with a red bac[k] ground; and a red instructor's lanyard is attached [to] the left breast pocket. On the left breast pocket is t[he] armour qualification badge, and the OT SHER[UT] MIVTZA'IM (operational service pin) is worn on t[he] right breast pocket. The SIKAT ME'MEM (office[r] qualification pin) is worn on the left collar by officers after their graduation from the office[r] course. A Beretta M1951S is tucked into the oli[ve] waist belt in typical IDF fashion.

H2: Sergeant candidate, SAYERET GOLANI, 1969
This SAMAL (sergeant) wears the Battledress Class [A] uniform with the olive Class A blouse underneat[h]. By 1969 the Battledress Class As were virtual[ly] obsolete, to be replaced by the olive and kha[ki] variants (e.g. Plate H1). The GOLANI unit tag [is] worn, as are SAYERET GOLANI 'Flying Leopar[d]' wings and basic parachutist wings. The khaki/gre[en] General Services beret was worn by GOLANI un[til] 1976. Nevertheless, SAYERET GOLANI wore bla[ck] headgear to differentiate themselves from oth[er] GOLANI infantrymen. Rank of squad lead[er] candidate is indicated by the blue tape backing [to] the infantry beret badge, and the shoulder str[ap] loops.

H3: Naval Commando, 1972
This KOMMANDO YAMI wears the white dr[ess] uniform, an exact copy of the Navy and Air For[ce] khaki Class A version, worn only on spec[ial]

A paratrooper loads his gear prior to a training jump, 1[9
Note manner in which GALIL ARM fits into weapons bag. ([IDF
Spokesman)

:asions. The Navy's blue beret with gold metal ʏʟ ʜᴀʏᴀᴍ (Navy) beret badge with light blue :ckground was standard Naval Class A headgear regular soldiers, NCOs, and officers until 1978, ien it was replaced by the white 'Popeye' hat for :ings, and white-topped peaked caps for NCOs d officers. The basic Naval Commando ᴋɴᴀꜰᴇɪ ᴀʟᴇɪꜰ ('bat wings') insignia is worn with red ombat) backing over the left breast pocket; while ister parachutist wings, indicating over 50 jumps, : worn with green backing above the right breast :cket. The rank of ʀᴀᴠ ꜱᴀᴍᴀʟ ʀɪꜱʜᴏɴ (First ister Sergeant) is indicated by the gold metal ord and wreath crest worn with red backing on a ick leather (Navy) watchband; the IDF uses a iversal ranking system for all services. The AK-47 th folding stock is this NCO's personal weapon; it ᴀplaced the ᴜᴢɪ as the Naval Commandos' issued eapon in the late 1960s, and has remained popular the unit to this day. Although attempts have been ide to standardise the ɢᴀʟɪʟ series in Naval ommando service, the 'captured' AKs evoke a rtain aura of élite status—besides being extremely ective combat weapons.

: *Commando*, ꜱᴀʏᴇʀᴇᴛ ᴍᴀᴛ'ᴋᴀʟ; *Beirut, 10 April 1973* though no photographs have been released from rael's spectacular commando raid on the Beirut adquarters of the 'Black September' organisation 10 April 1973, eyewitness accounts and official)F reports provide an accurate picture of what is actually worn. This commando of one of the ssassination teams', wears a black civilian rtleneck sweater and a black woollen cap. His ce, khaki canvas web gear (with pouches taped ut with black electrical tape for stealthy ovement), olive three-pocket fatigue trousers, and 7 small pack have all been greased black for lditional camouflage. An IMI M-26 fragmen- tion grenade and a K-Bar knife are worn on the stol belt. The ᴜᴢɪ 9mm SMG with folding stock is been fitted with an Israeli-produced silencer, id is supported by a khaki canvas sling specifically ᴇsigned for the ᴜᴢɪ, with integral slots for holding agazines.

: *Second Lieutenant*, ꜱᴀʏᴇʀᴇᴛ ɢᴏʟᴀɴɪ; *Mt. Hermon, 22 October 1973* his officer inching his way towards Syrian

entrenchments on the Israeli Hermon wears the 'Bar-Lev' spring jacket (named after the eighth IDF Chief of Staff, Lt.Gen. Haim Bar-Lev, who popularised its use) with insulated lining and white fur collar. The web gear consists of two ᴜᴢɪ magazine pouches, holding up to 20 magazines. Until 1973 the RPG-7 was issued to paratroop and commando units only (it is currently in general IDF service); like the RPG rocket bag, it is from captured Arab stocks.

I3: Recon paratrooper, ꜱᴀʏᴇʀᴇᴛ ꜱʜᴀᴋᴇᴅ; '*The Yard*', *16 October 1973* ꜱᴀʏᴇʀᴇᴛ ꜱʜᴀᴋᴇᴅ, the IDF Southern Command's paratroop reconnaissance battalion, was the 'elder statesman' of the territorial commando recon formations. During the 1973 War it was involved in fierce fighting against Egyptian commandos on both banks of the Suez Canal. This ꜱʜᴀᴋᴇᴅɴɪᴋ preparing to cross the Suez Canal into Egyptian Africa wears the 'German style' life vest, olive fatigue blouse and trousers, M-1 helmet fitted with tan netting supported by black rubber tubing, and brown paratrooper boots. A belt of 7.62mm ammunition for the FN MAG is worn across the chest, and two grenade pouches and a khaki canvas holster (secured to the leg by canvas strips) are worn on the pistol belt. Note the personal graffiti on the vest, ranging from a peace sign to his girlfriend's name.

A National Police sapper gingerly examines a suspicious parcel in Tel Aviv's 'Kings of Israel' Square, January 1986. The Police sappers answer 3,000 such calls annually, and during Israel's involvement in Lebanon were attached to the ʏᴀ'ᴍᴀ'ᴍ. A number were decorated for bravery, some of them posthumously. (Author's collection)

Naval Commando wings, *top to bottom:* **Underwater Demolitions Unit, Naval Commando (Basic), Naval Commando (Master). (Author's collection)**

J1: Recon infantryman, SAYERET GOLANI; Kfar Sil, 22 June 1982

Seen here with a souvenir portrait of PLO Chairman Yasir Arafat, he wears the IDF load-bearing system or EPHOD, a direct result of experience with the 'commando web gear' of the 1967–70 War of Attrition. The final product is an ingenious and extremely comfortable system, allowing the user to add or remove rear pouches at will. Underneath the EPHOD an Orlite-produced Kevlar flak vest is worn, as are the issue brown/khaki undershirt, here with long sleeves removed, and American OG-107 fatigue trousers. The weapon is the Israeli-produced GALIL 5.56mm ARM, which replaced the FN FAL, UZI, and M-16 as the most important infantry weapon in IDF use. US LAW 66mm anti-tank rockets are carried, with

a specially produced LAW carrying pack. By 19[?] the old copies of the US M-1 helmet had be[en] replaced by the lightweight Kevlar infantry ballist[ic] helmets, fitted here with tan netting, black rubb[er] tubing, and a red stencil of the unit emblem, th[e] 'Flying Leopard'.

J2: YA'MA'M Border Guard sniper, July 1982

Although the Border Guards possess a fatigue sh[irt] with MISHMAR HAGVUL ('Border Guard') nam[e] tape, their military equipment is identical to th[at] supplied to IDF soldiers. This anti-terrorist snip[er] preparing an ambush wears the Border Gua[rd] fatigue blouse and olive three-pocket fatig[ue] trousers. The Achidatex Ltd. AC-T Kevlar 'an[ti-] terrorist' bulletproof vest can be worn with [or] without additional protective ceramic plate[s] affording protection even against armour-pierci[ng] bullets. The vest has four ammunition pockets, tw[o] front and two rear; a front grenade pouch, and [a] rear canteen pouch. A Motorola walkie-talkie h[as] been placed in the front ammunition pouch, and [a] khaki canvas pistol belt supports a holster for [a] Beretta M1951S, and a Gerber commando kni[fe.] The M-16 5.56mm assault rifle has been fitted wi[th] a AN/PVS-4 sniper-scope and a 30-round ma[g]azine.

J3: Recon paratrooper, SAYERET TZANHANIM; P[t.] E-Zut, 1985

The harsh winters in Lebanon prompted the IDF [to] issue protective clothing. Two such articles were t[he] HERMONIOT fur-lined winter boots, and the on[e]-piece BEGED HOREF insulated winter suit here wo[rn] under an issue OG protective rain smock. Th[e] recon paratrooper—operating from M113 APCs— presents a distinctively armoured crewma[n] appearance. He wears the Type 602 Kevlar armo[ured] crewman protective helmet (with blinker stro[be] light attached, as well as a pack of foreign cigarett[es] taped to the front for easy access). The load-beari[ng] equipment is a variation of the current EPHO[D] designed specifically for armoured crewmen, a[nd] called EPHOD HEYL SHIRION (Armoured Corps w[eb] gear). It consists of four frontal pouches similar [to] the 'ChiCom' type, and accommodates tw[o] rectangular canteens, providing the crewman wi[th] greater comfort while operating in the confines [of] an armoured vehicle. The stretcher, carri[ed]

tached to an infantry packboard, suggests that the
ldier has temporarily left the 'security' of the
[113. Note GLILON with M203 grenade launcher;
1d 'liberated' Russian TT-33 pistol tucked into
eb gear.

: Second Lieutenant, YA'MA'M, 1985
en here during a training exercise, this officer
ears the Border Guards' dark green beret with
ational Police badge. The Border Guard 'battle-
ess' jacket with green fur collar is worn with the
ISHMAR HAGVUL emblem sewn to the upper left
m, above the pen pocket. For protection against
ar gas the SHALON Type 80 gas mask is worn, as is
e IDF (note TZAHAL stencil) NBC warfare bag
rapped to the left leg. The police rank of
EFAKEACH MISHNE is indicated by a small jewelled
if worn on green shoulder boards. The weapon is
e 9mm 'mini-UZI', a small version of the famous
I SMG which, although it has not been adopted
* the IDF, has undergone extensive testing in the
rder Guard.

*: Corporal, 50th NA'HA'L Paratroop Battalion; Hebron
1986*
rrying out the unpopular security duty on the
est Bank, he wears the olive fatigues and the
BON parka. The DUBON is extremely warm,
iterproof, and comfortable; the hood has slits for
e with headphones, and a pistol pocket is placed
ar the upper left sleeve. The KOVA RAFUL (named
er former Chief of Staff Lt.Gen. Rafael 'Raful'
an) fatigue hat with TZAHAL nametape is worn,
is an olive fatigue blouse and three-pocket fatigue
users. The rank of RABAT is indicated by two
ipes sewn on to the sleeves. An AN/PRC-77 field
lio is carried on the back in a tan-khaki canvas
cksack, the handset secured by the snug-fitting
b gear. The NA'HA'L tag is worn attached to the
t shoulder strap, and the paratrooper's red beret
ucked into the web gear. The GALIL 5.56mm AR
long-barrelled version of the GLILON SAR) is
rried, as is a bull-horn. The NA'HA'L maintains one
ratroop battalion, complete with a recon-
issance company, under the command of the
h Paratroop Bde.

: Senior master sergeant, SAYERET HADRUZIM, 1986
is RA'SA'B from the airborne-qualified and

Naval Commandos set out for a training operation near Atlit,
July 1986. Note black neoprene rubber diving suits, and
modified oxygen breathing system. (IDF Spokesman)

trained reconnaissance unit of the 300th Brigade
(the IDF's minority combat brigade, made up of
Druze Muslim conscripts as well as Bedouin,
Christian and Circassian volunteers) wears the
General Service Class A blouse, and paratroop
Class A three-pocket trousers—a combination well
within the restraints of regulations. Master parachutist wings with green backing are worn above
the left breast pocket, below which are worn the
SAYERET HADRUZIM recon wings, and a row of the
1967, 1973 and 1982 Lebanon campaign ribbons.
The 'woolly pully' sweater entered IDF service
following the 1982 Lebanon War when thousands
were captured; it is seen here modified with a frontal
zipper fitted with a grenade pin. Rank is indicated
by the gold-embroidered red cloth patch sewn on
both sleeves. The CAR-15 5.56mm assault rifle is
the favoured weapon of paratroop and infantry
NCOs and officers.

L1: Paratroop jump instructor, Tel Nof, 1987
The rank of master sergeant has always carried a
negative reputation; and it was felt that the highly
visible 'watchband ranks' contributed to this image.
As a result, on Independence Day 1986, the IDF
officially changed the rank insignia for all these
NCOs from the large metal insignia worn on the left
wrist to smaller, more discreet rank badges worn on
the collar, with a red backing for Army, light blue

The next generation of IDF élite, a GIVA'ATI Brigade SHU'ALEI SHIMSHON unit assaults a target in manoeuvres against the GOLANI Brigade in the Negev Desert. Note soldier carrying GLILON SAR with added forward pistol grip, and sniper in background firing an M-21. (IDF Spokesman)

for Air Force, and dark blue for Navy. This MADRICH TZNICHA (jump instructor) wears the paratroop Class A blouse, incorporating an olive waist belt. Master parachutist wings are worn above the left breast pocket, and HALO jump wings below the left collar, both with white backing indicating instructor status. The Lebanon ribbon is worn above the left breast pocket, and the operational service pin on the right breast pocket. Attached to the left shoulder strap is the unit tag for the Paratroop Jump School; the red beret, infantry beret badge, and brown boots are all universal paratrooper items. The white long-sleeved under-shirt is the issue 'winter sleeping garment', worn here as a 'fashionable' T-shirt.

L2: First Lieutenant, Air Force Aeromedical Evacuation Unit, 1987

The men of the Aeromedical Evacuation Unit are responsible for the immediate and successful rescue of any downed pilot, or combat soldiers trapped deep in enemy territory. Completely airmobile with a variety of helicopters, their most effective weapon

is speed, and the ability to operate in a topographical or climatic environment. They a familiar with every weapon in the enem possession, and are experts in hand-to-ha combat, quick infiltration, and extraction—ev cross-country skiing!

This SEGEN wears the Air Force khaki Class uniform, with a grey/blue officer's waist belt w silver metal buckle. The grey/blue officer's peak cap is worn, with silver metal HEYL HAVIR (A Force) badge with red backing. Like the Air Fo pilot wings, the AEU wings are embroidered silver on a dark blue cloth base, and worn over t left breast pocket. Rank is indicated by two silv metal bars, identical to the Army ranks, worn or grey/blue shoulder board without any backi Note officer's qualification pin worn on the l collar. The personal weapon is the AKMS 7.62m assault rifle, supported by a black canvas sling.

L3: Sergeant, SHU'ALEI SHIMSHON, 1987

When the GIVA'ATI Infantry Brigade was 'reborn' 1983 out of the remnants of SAYERET SHAKED as t IDF's version of a marine infantry force, the emergence of its historical reconnaissance un SHU'ALEI SHIMSHON ('Samson's Foxes') was inev able. Although originally issued with black bere when GIVA'ATI emerged as the élite IDF infant

nation—outperforming both the paratroopers
l the GOLANI in mock combat exercises—they
e awarded the honour of their own distinctive
ple beret. The Intelligence Corps badge worn
h red backing on the beret indicates that this
'ALEI SHIMSHON sergeant is attached an In-
igence unit. SHU'ALEI SHIMSHON recon wings
h green backing are worn over the left breast
ket, and the GIVA'ATI Brigade unit pin is
ached to the left pocket; a green instructor's
yard is fastened to it. The GLILON 5.56mm SAR
en here fitted with a forward pistol grip, and
ded with the unusual 50-round magazine. A
retta M92 9mm pistol is tucked into the olive
st belt. Note IDF-issue kit bag.

Aeromedical Evacuation Unit Bell 212 pilot displays his
erican K-2B sage green flight suit, dark green SPH-4C
le-visor helmet, and Israeli-produced survival gear
hes. (Herzl Kunesari-IDF Spokesman)

es sur les planches en couleur

ombinaison d'articles britanniques, civils et HAGANAH, dont la casquette de
turc de la *Jewish Settlement Police*. Le fusil Lewis peu courant n'est utilisé que
les grandes batailles. **A2** Blouse de camouflage de l'ancienne 6ème Division
portée britannique, étuis de munitions de l'armée des Etats-Unis et pantalons
. Le fusil Lee Enfield, le pistolet P38 et la grenade se complètent d'un lance-
mes de fabrication IRGUN. **A3** Le dispositif lance-grenades du fusil et le 'fusil
sont de fabrication HAGANAH.

abit israélien et insigne de parachutiste TZAHAL; le reste de la tenue est de
cation britannique, à l'exception de la mitraillette MP40. **B2** Ancien
rme copié sur une tenue de combat britannique. A noter l'insigne de
chutiste brodé remplacé par un insigne en métal à partir de 1953.
arquer les galons de sergent rudimentaires, le ruban de la campagne de 1948
fusil tchèque K98. **B3** Tenue de combat standard portée en guise d'uniforme
'au milieu des années soixante-dix; l'écusson de l'unité de métier de
chutistes est ici cousu sur la manche au lieu d'être porté sous la forme d'un
amovible; le col est orné de deux insignes TZAHAL et les pattes d'épaule
ignes de grade en bronze placées les unes comme les autres sur un fond rouge.
ordon rouge désigne les instructeurs.

Cette unité portait une gamme bigarrée d'habits et de matériels
uipement: dans ce cas, un couvre-chef de type britannique, une blouse de
ouflage britannique et des pantalons israéliens. La copie insraélienne d'un sac
nnique renferme une réserve de munitions pour un fusil Bren. **C2** Autre
nge caractéristique d'habits et de matériel, de fabrication en grande partie
ienne, à l'exception du foulard arabe porté comme une écharpe. **C3**
ments israéliens, mélange de matériel britannique et des USA et dispositif
-grenades sur le fusil K98.

ujourd'hui beaucoup plus élégant, l'uniforme est de fabrication entièrement
lienne à l'exception du casque britannique. Remarquer l'étui pour dix
asins, une ancienne mitraillette UZI et un pistolet 0.38 Smith & Wesson dans
fourreau. **D2** Uniforme et matériel d'équipement israélien standard,
rrenant des étuis pour les magasins FN FAL; copie de sac britannique
rmant des gamelles dont les couvercles servent souvent à porter des
ades. **D3** Habit de camouflage 'lézard' de provenance française, casque et
chutes de type américain; le grand sac d'armes renferme un bazooka de 3.5 in.
brication locale, et le petit l'UZI, sous le parachute de réserve.

enue de camouflage 'lézard' portée par-dessus une veste au col de fourrure;
pour magasins et grenades UZI; pistolet M1951 Beretta dans son fourreau. **E2**
de campagne M1943 américaine et uniforme de camouflage français; radio
PRC-10 sur le 'packboard' de l'infanterie; casque britannique. **E3** La
iller léger porte cet anorak que les Israéliens appellent 'battledress', ici sans
anches, par-dessus un uniforme de camouflage 'lézard'; les touches
onnelles telles que celle-ci étaient courantes parmi les unités d'élite.

'uniforme de 'Classe A' conforme de façon à ne pas surprendre les civils.
oupe de la veste (et des pantalons) est particulière aux troupes de
chutistes (et GOLANI). Tous les parachutistes engagés portent un insigne sur
bleu; remarquer également le ruban de la campagne de 1967. De

Farbtafeln

A1 Kombination britischer, ziviler und HAGANAH-Stücke, inkl. Kappe der Jewish
Settlement Police in türkischem Stil. Das seltene Lewis-Gewehr würde nur in
grossangelegten Gefechten riskiert werden. **A2** Tarnkittel, ex-britisch, 6.
Airborne Division, US-Armme-Munitionsgürtel und Zivilhosen. Das Lee
Enfield-Gewehr, die P 38-Pistole und Granate werden durch einen von IRGUN
hergestellten Flammenwerfer ergänzt. **A3** Die Granatwerfervorrichtung auf dem
Gewehr und das Sten-Maschinengewehr wurden von der HAGANAH hergestellt.

B1 Israelische Kleidung, und TZAHAL-Fallschirmjägerabzeichen; Rest der
Ausrüstung ist britischer herkunft, abgesehen von der MP40-Maschinenpistole.
B2 Frühe formelle Uniform, der britischen kampuniform nachgemacht; siehe
gesticktes Fallschirmjägerabzeichen, 1953 durch Metallabzeichen ersetzt. Siehe
grobe Gefreitenstreifen, Band für Feldzug 1948 und tschechisches K98-Gewehr.
B3 Standard-Felduniform, als formelle Uniform getragen bis Mitte der 70er
Jahre; Schulterabzeichen der regulären Fallschirmjägereinheit ist hier am Ärmel
aufgenäht, anstatt als abnehmbare Klappe getragen; am Kragen zwei TZAHAL-
Abzeichen, auf den Schulterklappen bronzene Rangabzeichen, beide auf rotem
Grund. Die rote Schnur kennzeichnet Instruktor.

C1 Diese Einheit trug eine bunte Auswahl von Kleidungsstücken und
Ausrüstung: in diesem Falle eine britische Kappe, britischen Tarnkittel und
israelische Hosen. Die israelische Kopie britischer Gurten enthält Re-
servemunition für eine Bren-Maschinenpistole. **C2** Ebenfalls eine typische
Mischung von Kleidungsstücken und Ausrüstung, hauptsächlich israelischer
Herkunft, abgesehen von dem arabischen Kopftuch, als Halstuch getragen. **C3**
Israelische Kleidung, Mischung aus britischer und US-Ausrüstung, israelische
Granatwerfervorrichtung auf dem K98-Gewehr.

D1 Jetzt schon viel eleganter—die Uniform ist rein israelisch, abgesehen vom
britischen helm. Siehe Gurt für 10 Magazine, frühe UZI-Maschinenpistole, Pistole
Smith & Wesson .38 in Halfter. **D2** Israelische Standarduniform und Ausrüstung,
inkl. Gurten für FN FAL-Magazine; kopierter britischer Sprengstoffbeutel;
Feldflaschen, deren Hüllen oft zur Aufbewahrung von Granaten verwendet
werden. **D3** Lizard-Tarnkleidung französischer herkunft, Helm amerikanischer
Art und Fallschirme; der grössere Waffenbehälter enthält eine lokal angefertigte
3,5 Zoll-Bazooka, der kleiner unter dem Reservefallschirm die UZI.

E1 Lizard-Tarnanzug über Jacke mit Penzkragen; Gurten für UZI-Magazine
und Granaten; gehalfterte Beretta M1951-Pistole. **E2** US-Feldjacke M1943 und
französische Tarnuniform; AN/PRC-10-Funkgerät auf Infanterie-Packboard;
britischer helm. **E3** Dieser leichte Maschinengewehrschütze trägt die israelische
sog. Battledress-Windjacke, hier mit abgeschnittenen Ärmeln, über Lizard-
Tarnuniform; solche persönlichen Variationen waren unter den Elite-Einheiten
üblich.

F1 'Class A'—Uniform wurde getragen, um die Zivilbevölkerung nicht zu
erschrecken! Der Schnitt der jacke und Hosen ist typisch für die Fallschirmjäger-
und GOLANI-Truppen. Alle regulären Paras tragen Schwingen auf blauem
Grund; siehe auch das Band für den Feldzug 1967. Viele Eliteeinheiten tragen
AK-47 Gewehre. **F2** Die Arbeitsbluse mit gelbem TZAHAL-Aufdruck und
Arbeitskappe wurden nach dem Krieg von 1967 allgemein getragen. Er trägt

nombreuses unités d'élite ont des fusils AK-47. **F2** La tenue de corvée décorée de lettres TZAHAL jaunes, et la casquette assortie, se répandirent après la guerre de 1967. Ce soldat porte des armes et des étuis saisis à l'ennemi ou copiés sur ceux de l'ennemi; ses explosifs sont dans un sac vert en nylon. **F3** Veste teinte en ocre pour ressembler à l'uniforme égyptien; les explosifs se trouvent sur le 'packboard'; prototype de matériel d'équipement léger, aujourd'hui de fabrication standard mais réalisé à l'origine par les parachutistes à partir de tissu d'uniforme; et remarquer les genouillères.

G1 A noter le matériel d'équipement imperméable mis au point pour les commandos navals. **G2** La plupart des soldats israéliens ont deux spécialités de combat; cet homme porte à la fois un étui médical et des grenades anti-personnel et antichar. Remarquer le clignotant fixé au casque pour les opérations nocturnes. **G3** Veste de terrain M-65 et pantalons OG-107 américains, casque de type américain et de fabrication locale, et matériel d'équipement doublé de caoutchouc mousse. **G4** Tireur d'élite de cette unité secrète qui se prépare à délivrer des otages retenus dans un avion de ligne détourné; il porte un combinaison blanche de mécanicien aéronautique et il est armé d'un Beretta M1951.

H1 Cet homme porte le béret et l'insigne du corps blindé, l'insigne de parachutiste ainsi que celle, propre à cette unité, représentant un char ailé sur le fond vert de toutes les unités de reconnaissance. A noter l'insigne de grade d'officier sur la partie gauche du col, celui de grade au sein du corps blindé sur la poche gauche et celui du service opérationnel sur la poche droite. **H2** Insigne d'unité GOLANI sur l'épaule de la tenue de combat 'Classe A', presque obsolète en 1969; béret noir SAYERET GOLANI et, sur la poitrine, insigne d'unité de reconnaissance représentant un léopard volant; le candidat sous-officier se reconnaît à une ganse bleue qui orne son béret et ses pattes d'épaule. **H3** Uniforme de cérémonie et béret porté par la marine avant 1978. L'insigne 'en ailes de chauve-souris' du commando de la marine possède un fond rouge qui indique un service de combat, alors que celui 'en ailes de parachute' a le fond vert des unités de reconnaissance. L'insigne de grade se porte au poignet, sur un bracelet montre.

I1 Selon des témoins oculaires, ce costume à moitié civil aurait été porté lors de ce raid nocturne. Remarquer l'UZI accompagné d'un silencieux. **I2** Veste dite 'Bar-Lev' d'après le nom du général qui en répandit l'utilisation. Les RPG-7 sont désormais communs. **I3** Brassière de sauvetage de style allemand utilisée pour franchir le canal de Suez.

J1 L'équipement EPHOD, que les commandos ont été les premiers à utiliser (Voir F3), est désormais standard; il est ici porté par-dessus le gilet pare-balles *Kevlar*. A cette date, le casque *Kevlar* avait remplacé l'ancien casque de type américain; à remarquer l'insigne du 'léopard volant'; les armes sont un fusil GALIL ARM et des fusées des Etats-Unis LAW-66. **J2** Mélange d'uniforme de garde-frontières et d'équipement militaire; le gilet pare-balles AC-T 'anti-terroriste' peut recevoir des plaques céramiques en vue d'une protection accrue, et ses étuis peuvent renfermer des munitions et une radio, en cas de besoin. **J3** La tenue d'hiver et les bottes mises au point pour les opérations menées au Liban par temps froid s'accompagnent ici d'une veste imperméable; le casque et le matériel d'équipement ici d'une veste imperméable; le casque et le matériel d'équipement sont destinés tout particulièrement aux équipes d'appareils transporteurs blindés. Cet homme porte un fusil GLILON accompagné d'un lance-grenades et, sur son dos, un brancard.

K1 Béret et insigne de garde-frontières, et veste *battledress* verte avec écusson de garde-frontières; masque à gaz et trousse chimique sur la jambe gauche; insigne de rang sur les pattes d'épaule, et 'mini-UZI' propre aux gardes-frontières. **K2** L'insigne HAHAL sur la manche désigne cette unité de la 35ème brigade parachutiste; noter la parka d'hiver DUBON, le fusil GALIL AR et la radio AN/PRC-77. **K3** L'unité de reconnaissance de la 300ème brigade, constituée de races minoritaires, possède un insigne spécial en forme d'ailes que ses membres portent ici au-dessous de l'insigne de parachutiste; remarquer le pullover à fermeture éclair, le fusil CAR-15 et l'insigne de grade cousu sur les poignets.

L1 Nouvel insigne de rang de 1986: placé au col, il remplace celui de type bracelet-montre. Le maître-parachute et les ailes HALO sont placés sur le fond blanc de l'insigne de l'instructeur; l'écusson désigne l'Ecole de saut en parachute. **L2** Uniforme 'Classe A' de l'armée de l'air avec, sur la poitrine gauche, l'insigne de l'Unité d'évacuation aéromédicale, et l'insigne de grade habituel. **L3** L'insigne du Service de renseignments porté sur le nouveau béret violet de la brigade GIVA'ATI indique que l'homme appartient au sein du renseignements au sein de la brigade. Le cordon vert de l'instructeur s'attache à l'insigne GIVA'ATI épinglé sur la poitrine en-dessous des ailes de reconnaissance de cette unité.

Waffen und Gurten, die vom Feind erbeutet oder kopiert wurden, und Spreng- in einem grünen Nylonsack. **F3** Braun gefärbte Jacke soll ägyptische Unif vortäuschen; Sprengstoffe auf Packboard getragen; Prototyp leichter Gurtaus tung, jetzt Standardausrüstung, aber ursprünglich von Fallschirmjäg selbstverfertigt aus Uniformstoff; siehe Kneeschützer.

G1 Siehe spezielle wasserdichte Ausrüstung für Marinekommandos. **G2** meisten israelischen Soldaten haben zwei Einsatzspezialitäten; dieser Mann t sowohl einen Medizinbeutel sowie Splitter und Panzerabwehrgranaten. S Blinklicht am Helm für Nachteinsätze. **G3** US-M-65-Feldjacke und OG-I Hosen, lokal hergestellter Helm nach US-Art; Gurten mit Schaumgur gepolstert. **G4** Der Scharfschütze dieser geheimen Abteilung ist im begi Geiseln in einem entführten Flugzeug zu retten; er trägt weissen Overall e Flugzeugmechanikers und ist mit Beretta M1951 bewaffnet.

H1 Panzerkorps-Kappe mit Abzeichen, ausserdem Fallschirmjägerschwin und das spezielle Panzerabzeichen dieser Einheit auf dem grünen Grund a Aufklärungseinheiten. Siehe Offizierspatentabzeichen auf der linken Kra seite; Panzerabzeichen, linke Tasche, und Einsatzabzeichen, rechte Tas **H2** Abzeichen der GOLANI-Einheit auf der Schulter der 'Class A'-Battledress, 1969 fast überflüssig geworden; schwarze Kappe SAYERET GOLANI, Aufklärungsschwinge 'Fliegender Leopard' auf der Brust; Unteroffizierskand gekennzeichnet durch auf Kappe und Schulterspange. **H3** Formelle Unif und Kappe der Marine vor 1978. Blaues Fledermausflü Kommandoabzeichen auf rotem Grund zeigt Kampfeinsatz an; P Schwingenauf grünem Aufklärergrund. Rangabzeichen auf Uhrarmb getragen.

I1 Augenzeugenberichten zufolge wurde dieses halbzivile Kostüm bei di nächtlichen Angriff getragen. Siehe UZI mit Schalldämpfer. **I2** Die Sog. Bar-I Jacke, nach dem general, der ihre Verwendung populär machte. RPG-7 jetzt allgemein getragen. **I3** Schwimmweste deutscher Art wird beim Überse des Suezkanals getragen.

J1 Die EPHOD-Ausrüstung, von den Kommandos (siehe F3) eingeführt, gehör Standardausrüstung, hier über der Kevlar-Panzerweste getragen. Der Kev Helm hat jetzt den früheren US-artigen Helm ersetzt—siehe Aufdruck Abzeichens 'Fliegender Leopard'; GALIL ARM-Gewehr und US LAW Raketen. **J2** Mischung aus Grenzwache-Uniform und Armeeausrüstung; AC-T-Panzerweste gegen Terroristen kann zusätzliche Keramikplatten auf men für grösseren Schutz, und in den Gurten kann Munition und Funkg getragen werden. **J3** Winteranzug und Stiefel für Kaltwettereinsätze im Liba mit Regenjacke; Helm und Gurten für die besatzung gepanzerter Tr pentransporter. Er trägt ein GLILON-Gewehr mit Granatwerfer, und am Rüc eine Bahre.

K1 Grenzwache-Kappe und Abzeichen und grüne Battledress-Jacke Grenzwache-Schulterabzeichen; Gasmaske und Ausrüstung für chemi Kriegführung in Beutel am linken Bein; Rangabzeichen auf Schulterspan Mini-UZI, typisch für Grenzwachen. **K2** NAHAL-Abzeichen am Ärmel identifi diese Einheit der 35. Para-Brigade; siehe DUBON-Pelzjacke, GALIL AR-Gev und AN/PRC-77-Funkgerät. **K3** Die Aufklärungseinheit der 300.Brigade, völkischen Minoritäten zusammengesetzt, mit spezieller Schwinge unter Para-Schwingen; siehe Pullover mit Reissverschluss, CAR-15-Gewehr aufgenähte Rangabzeichen an den Manschetten.

L1 Neue Rangabzeichen (1986) am Kragen ersetzen die Armbandabzeic Schwingen für geübten Fallschirmjäger und HALO auf dem weissen Grund Instruktors getragen; Schulterabzeichen identifiziert Fallschirmjägerschule. 'Class-A'-Luftwaffeuniform mit Schwinge der Aeromedical Evacuation -Ein links an der Brust, normale Rangabzeichen. **L3** Nachrichtendienstabzeic getragen auf den neuen, violetten Kappe der GIVA'ATI-Brigade, zeigt nachrichtendiensteinheit der Brigade an. Grüne Schnur des Instruktors is GIVA'ATI-Abzeichen an der Brust unterhalb der Aufklärungsschwinge d Einheit befestigt.